Oh, What a Beautiful Lady!

1SBN 0 85172 760 3 Paperback

Nihil obstat R. J. Cumming DD
Censor

Imprimatur David Norris

Westminster, 23. VII. 1976

The Nihil obstat *and* Imprimatur *are a declaration that a book or pamphlet is considered to be free from doctrinal or moral error. It is not implied that those who have granted the* Nihil obstat *and* Imprimatur *agree with the contents, opinions or statements expressed.*

Printed by
Samuel Walker Limited, Hinckley, Leics
From text set by
Cardinal Press, London
and published by
AUGUSTINE PUBLISHING COMPANY
South View, Chawleigh,
Chulmleigh, Devon, EX18 7HL

Oh, What a Beautiful Lady!

The Message of Fatima

by

DAMIEN WALNE & JOAN FLORY

DEVON MCMLXXVI

ACKNOWLEDGMENTS

The authors are indebted to the Memoirs and Letters of Sister Lucy for the source material on which this book is based.

The picture of Jacinta on the front cover is reproduced by kind permission of Casa Jacinta Marto, Portugal.

DEDICATION

We dedicate this book
to our dear
Father L. Cuthbert Smith, O.S.B.

CONTENTS

LIST OF ILLUSTRATIONS

FOREWORD

By The Most Reverend J. A. Murphy, Archbishop of Cardiff

Anyone who has been at Fatima on Pilgrimage day and witnessed the conclusion of the Pilgrimage with a sea of handkerchiefs waving their mass adieux to Our Lady of Fatima will realise that the Portuguese have a lively and homely way of expressing their affection. A little sticky and emotional, you may think, but it is not just candy floss. There's substance there.

Can I illustrate this from a piece of modern history which concerns one of their national patrons—St. Anthony of Lisbon? (In Lisbon, you refer to him at your peril as St. Anthony of Padua. He is not for export).

The scene is Brazil, the year just about 1917 when Our Lady appeared at Fatima. A famous court case is being heard, with learned judges and military arguing the case, and in the dock, for better or for worse, St. Anthony. Can I briefly sketch the circumstances which led to that court case? It shows something of the substance which underlies the devotion of the Portuguese to their patrons.

A regiment in Portugal chose St. Anthony as their patron. He is immediately entered in their pay-book as Private St. Anthony, and each week he drew his pay, which was handed over to St. Anthony's bread and given to the poor. Later this same regiment was saved almost by chance from a perilous ambush. They immediately attributed their escape to Private St. Anthony, and in recognition advanced him to the rank of Sergeant St. Anthony and increased his pay accordingly.

After several years as a sergeant, a plea was made that Sergeant St. Anthony had served the regiment with honour, and impeccably, without any loss of stripes, and that therefore his majority be recognised. The plea was accepted and he became Captain St. Anthony, with the appropriate rise in salary. Subsequently he climbed to Colonel of the regiment. But at this time both Portugal and Brazil—which as an original Portuguese colony had adopted Colonel St. Anthony––had fallen into a recession, and economies had to be made. Colonel St. Anthony was placed on the reserve and his salary docked to half pay.

Hence the court case in Brazil in 1917, and the question before the court was: Now that Brazil had entered the war on the side of the allies, what about reservist St. Anthony? Shouldn't he be called up and placed with the others on the active list, and restored to full pay?

My researches never discovered the ultimate findings of that court, but I would put my money on Colonel St. Anthony and the logic which underlies the apparent flossy nature of their devotion.

Reading the translations of original Portuguese reports on Fatima, upon which this book is based, you might be tempted to see in them a similar superficial whimsicality. But they are all underpinned with a solid and innate devotion to the Mother of God. The Portuguese effervesce, but they keep their powder dry.

This reminds me so much of Bernadette, who on her second or third visit to meet the Lady armed herself with a bottle of holy water and sprinkled her with it, just in case she had any connection with the Devil. The Lady smiled, we are told. What else could she do? And both the Lady and St. Bernadette resumed the telling of their beads. Another similarity with Lourdes: The message from both apparitions was the same––Prayer and Penance.

The world would be a little more substantial if we had both. And incidentally, I have always thought that the ecumenical movement would move a little faster if we had the Mother of God.

+ John Murphy
Archbishop of Cardiff

AUTHORS' INTRODUCTION

Portugal is an oblong strip of land 360 miles long and varying from 80 to 140 miles wide.

Despite being part of the Iberian Massif, it has existed as a separate nation with the same frontiers for over 800 years.

1139 is regarded as the foundation year of the Kingdom of Portugal, when a winning battle against the Moors at Ourique resulted in most of Portugal being liberated.

The land south of the river Tagus, however, was not cleared of Moors until the almost impregnable fortress of Alcacer de Sol fell in 1217, and this only after many years of fruitless attempts.

It was after one such failure, so legend has it, that a raiding party, led by Don Conçalvo Henriques, captured the Moorish governor of the fort's daughter: improbable as it may seem, they fell in love.

Consent for their marriage was given on condition that she became a Christian. This she did, changing her name from Fatima, so called after Mohammed's daughter, to Oureana. The fief given them by the king lay in the hills south-east of Leiria and was later called Ourem after her.

Within a year of marrying, Oureana died. Heartbroken, Don Conçalvo gave up his possessions and retired to the monastery at Alcobaca, but not before building an elaborate chapel on the opposite mountain, in which he buried his wife. He named the chapel Fatima and it is on this site that the present church in Fatima stands.

Even with the Moors' expulsion, this newly founded kingdom was always threatened with invasion from neighbouring Castille. The battle that finally ensured Portugal's independence from Spain and established a dynasty that remained until the present century was at Aljubarrota in 1385. Under the command of Nun'Alvares

Perreira, an army, despite being greatly outnumbered by Castillians, gained a memorable victory, to which the magnificent Gothic monastery at Batalha, dedicated to Our Lady of Victories, stands as a memorial and today houses the tomb of the unknown soldier.

Since the Moors were driven out, Portugal has remained ostensibly a Catholic country. Its people are God-fearing; seafarers and tillers of the soil, they know all about the vagaries of the climate with its history of treacherous seas and storms, earthquakes, heat, droughts and floods. All of which has given them a healthy respect for the supernatural.

Outstanding among devotions is love of the Mother of God, who is patroness of their country. For three hundred years the kings of Portugal, until the last was expelled, never wore their crowns, but laid them at the feet of Mary, Queen of Portugal. Both men and women alike are able to identify with her who, although a virgin, was a mother who knows about family hardships and the rigours of work on the land. Every village has its patron virgin, and on her feast days streets are festooned with garlands of flowers and coloured paper, while her statue covered with carnations and roses can be seen tottering and swaying to the rhythm of her bearers' footsteps: the music of the bands is both festive and melancholy.

In fact so deep rooted is this love of Our Lady that there are very few Portuguese women who are not called after her. The name Maria can be seen burned into ceramic pottery, carved on the elegant Phoenician shaped prows of fishing vessels or cut into the flowery designs of oxen yokes, embroidered on lace, even written in cinnamon on bread.

The saints and angels too have their place in Portuguese life and like Our Lady are treated as friends and helpers. People call upon St. Anthony, for instance, to find their lost possessions; St. Rita is a defender of hopeless causes; in fact, there is a saint to cover every contingency. Guardian angels are prayed to for protection, and it is customary for small girls dressed as angels to accompany the processions on the major feast days, even though at the close of festivities their dresses are dirty, halos crooked and wings drooping!

So it is not at all strange that the appearance of Our Lady at Fatima should fan the flame of an already deep rooted love and effect such a national reponse on the big occasions from May to October when lines of pilgrims cover all the roads leading to this village in the remote mountains of the Serra D'Aire.

JACINTA
FRANCISCO
LÚCIA

CHAPTER ONE

"I WANT TO BE WITH LUCY....."

"Oh Mama Mama," Jacinta whined, "why can't I have my own sheep?""

"For the umpteenth time NO, you're far too young."

The child tugged at her mother's full skirted dress. "But Mama I'm not, I'm six years old, anyway Francisco'll come with me, and he's nearly eight."

Glaring at her daughter the woman raised her voice. "Will you get out of the way? You can see I'm busy."

"It's not fair," the youngster said defiantly, "Lucy was only a bit older than me when she took out uncle Antonio's sheep."

This was met with silence, and realising she was getting nowhere, Jacinta stomped from the kitchen and went to her brother's room, where he sat quietly carving a flute.

"For goodness sake, Francisco, stop that stupid job and persuade Mama to let us go to the fields with Lucy." The boy raised his head and regarded the elfin like figure before him; her usually pallid face was flushed, and the brown eyes smouldered with annoyance.

"Hurry up." Jacinta poked his shoulder.

"I don't want to go out with Lucy, or sheep, come to that," he replied tranquilly.

"You wouldn't." The braids of fair hair swung as she tossed her head, "you only ever want to be on your own, now do as I say or I'll take that silly flute from you." She made a grab but her brother was quicker, and without another word, stood up, and went to the kitchen.

"Mama, can Jacinta and me have some sheep and go with Lucy?"

Olympia Marto was a gentle woman by nature but now she was irritated. For the past few weeks she had been pestered unceasingly. Not only did she consider her daughter too young to take care of sheep, but they already had a flock which twelve year old John tended daily; to buy more would simply be satisfying the whim of a child. Now here she was, confronted by a slightly taller replica of her youngest.

"Oh, so that young madam's got you at it, has she? Well you can tell her the answer is no, she's wasting her time."

"Alright, Mama," he said indifferently, "it doesn't matter to me. I'm not all that keen on Lucy even though she is our cousin."

Francisco returned to his room where Jacinta waited impatiently.

"What she say, what she say?"

"No, of course, what did you expect?" Shrugging her shoulders, the little thing said, "Oh well, I'll worry about it later, it's time to go and meet Lucy now, come on...."

Francisco followed and within minutes the pair were making their way along the stony road to Lucy's home at the other end of the village. Outside the house they waited, drinking in the beauty of the setting sun. In its rosy glow windmills dotting the surrounding hills stood out and appeared to be very much nearer. At the tinkle of sheep bells, Jacinta turned and ran to greet her cousin who approached with the flock.

"Oh Lucy, Lucy," she kissed the older girl, "I've missed you so much. I wish we had more time to play together.... I keep asking Mama to let us come with you, but she always says no."

"Well there's time for a game now.....come and help me bed the sheep......Francisco", Lucy raised her voice, "you too."

An old threshing floor at the top of the house served as a playground; the trio chased around, rolling and tumbling, until exhausted they sat and gave their attention to the sky. Looking at the moon Jacinta exclaimed, "Our Lady's lamp is burning brightly tonight," then pointing to the stars, "and look how many angel's lamps are lit."

"Hmm, they're lovely," Lucy answered, "I know, let's see who can count the most... one, two, three...are you counting Francisco?"

"No," the boy said dreamily, "I was thinking about the sun, no lamp is as beautiful as Our Lord's."

It was the loud authoritative voice of Lucy's mother that stopped their game.

"Oh dear," sighed Jacinta, "the time goes so quickly when we're playing. As soon as I get home I'll have a go at Papa. Mama won't give in but I bet I can persuade Papa to let us have some sheep, then Francisco and me can come with you to the pastures, won't that be lovely?"

Lucy grimaced, she was not too sure about that!

The Marto Home

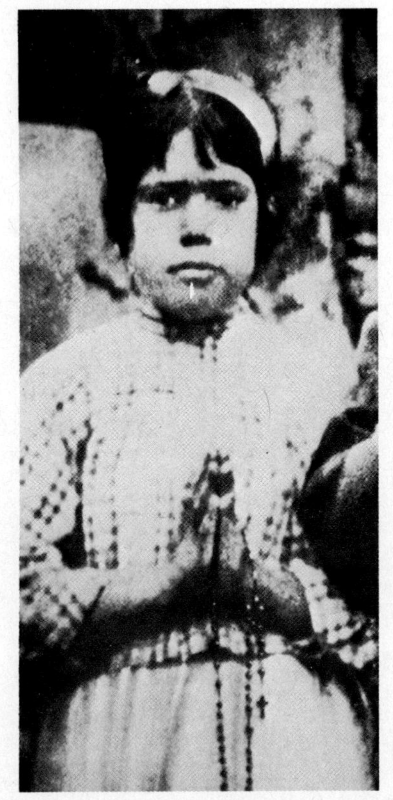

Lucy

CHAPTER TWO

THE SHEPHERDS' MASS

Maria-Rosa Santos shook her daughter, "Come on Lucy, it's time to get ready for Mass."

Her mother left the room and Lucy forced herself to consciousness, tossed back the covers and climbed out of bed.

She was rather on the big side though not yet nine years old. In complete contrast to her cousins Lucy was very plain; heavy features were accentuated by a large mouth with thick full lips; her lively personality and beautiful smile, however, more than compensated for this.

Now in the kitchen she showed her face the water and dressed. Her blue woollen skirt, which had been hand woven on the family loom, was topped with a sprigged flower-patterned blouse. Over her brown centre-parted hair she wore a colourful 'kerchief.

Though their features were alike, the mode of dress was not, and the young girl's outfit looked almost gaudy beside the sombre black of her mother's. No one could call Maria-Rosa feminine, and because of a stern and permanent care-worn expression, she looked older than her years.

Leaving the house they were joined by a handful of villagers, and within minutes sleepy Aljustrel was left behind, for apart from those who had flocks to pasture, Sunday was a day of rest, and most went to a later Mass.

Covering well trodden tracks which led to Fatima a half-mile distant, they were soon attending the Shepherds' Mass. When it was sermon time the priest said, "My dear people, this morning I'm just going to say a few words about the dreadful war that is raging." All eyes were riveted on him.

"Well, you know it's been going on for two years, since 1914, and," he said sadly, "it seems to be getting worse.

More countries are becoming involved; now I hear America has joined in...." He lowered his voice a little, "it's getting to the proportions of a world war, so terrible, there's even machines that fly spitting fire. I'm afraid some of our own boys will lose their lives...."

These words triggered off thoughts in Maria–Rosa's mind. Having five girls and only one son, she was worried lest her eldest follow his pals into the army. 'Things are bad enough,' she mused, 'with just him and his father working the land, but to be minus a pair of hands.'

This bothered her all through Mass, but by the time she reached home the daily round took precedence. While Lucy changed into her peasant smock, Maria-Rosa re-kindled the fire and prepared a frugal breakfast. After this the young shepherdess kissed her mother, took the bag containing a packed lunch, then set off with her sheep for the day.

When she returned that evening the family were talking about the war, a topic that ultimately took up most of the conversation at dinner.

"It must be bad," Maria-Rosa said, "for the Padre to give all his sermon time to talking about it.... I thought he looked under the weather too!"

"Hmm," her husband Antonio replied, "mind you, he's got far too much to do in this scattered parish; still the way things are going with the new government we're lucky to have a priest at all....they've already driven out most of the religious orders."

Lucy, busily eating, stopped momentarily. "New government, we're always having new governments!"

Completely ignoring her, Maria-Rosa went on, "I hear they've even stopped training men for the priesthood."

At this point the door suddenly burst open to admit Jacinta and Francisco, without so much as an 'excuse me', Jacinta said breathlessly, "Papa's given us some sheep of our own...we can go with Lucy tomorrow!"

CHAPTER THREE

"DO NOT BE AFRAID"

When Lucy arrived, her two cousins complete with sheep were waiting at the Barreiro pond where they had agreed always to meet.

"So....you managed to get up then!"

Francisco yawned and said sleepily, "I can't see why she wants to go out with sheep, it's almost the middle of the night!"

Looking at him scornfully, Jacinta turned to Lucy and asked, "Where are we going?"

"The Sierra, that's where all my friends'll be."

Jacinta's disappointment showed. "Do we have to? I thought we'd be just us three....anyway I want to go to the Cabeço."

Not wishing to become involved in an argument so early in the day the elder girl agreed. Carefully guiding the sheep past red sandy well cultivated plots of ground, they made their way to the private property owned by Lucy's godfather, and near an outcrop of rock they put their woolly charges to graze.

The mist of this lovely May morning had now dispersed and the children were content to sit for a while looking at the panorama. Below they could see their village, and to its right among a profusion of dark green trees peeped the white-washed houses of scattered hamlets. On the other side was a piece of grass-land called Valinhos, and beyond this in the distance a church spire well landmarked Fatima. To their left, stretching as far as the eye could see, was the rough shrubland of the Sierra, the main grazing area of the district.

It was not long before Francisco began to play the flute which he was never without. That did it! Jacinta was on her feet, promptly followed by Lucy, and within seconds they

The Cabeço

were dancing about in a clearing. This became too tame for Jacinta. "Faster, faster," she cried, "play something else." Her brother obliged and the tempo changed. Their antics would have continued had they not noticed the sheep straying.

Not too happy about the interruption Jacinta decided there and then to do something about it. As the days passed she hit on the idea of giving the animals tit-bits, thus encouraging them to stay close by; even with this problem solved there were not enough hours in the day for her games. Something had to suffer; it was their prayers. The custom was to say the rosary after lunch, but again the small girl's ingenuity paid off; by saying only the first two words of each prayer the rosary was over within minutes.

After saying the decades in this fashion one day at the Cabeco, they were startled by a sudden strong wind which shook the olive trees. Looking in this direction they saw a bright light moving towards them; when it stopped they perceived the radiant figure of a youth. Smiling at them he said, *"Don't be afraid, I am the Angel of Peace...pray with me."* He then prostrated himself on the ground.

When the flabbergasted children had done likewise he continued, *"Repeat after me, My God, I believe, I adore, I hope and I love you. I beg pardon for those who do not believe, do not adore, do not hope and do not love you."* Then rising he turned to them saying, *"You must pray much, the Hearts of Jesus and Mary are always attentive to you."* Then he vanished.

For a while the visitation was very much to the fore of the youngsters' minds, by the height of the summer, however, the euphoria had lifted and the angel was forgotten.

During these hot months the flocks were brought home before mid-day and taken out again in the cool of the evening, leaving the children free afternoons. After a brief siesta they always went to the well in the Santos garden, and there beneath the shade of fig and plum trees played undisturbed.

They were playing dib-stones one afternoon and, having run out of pebbles for which they were competing, resorted to using buttons; as a result Lucy's blouse was buttonless! Jacinta as usual had won, or rather, the other two, in order to avoid a tantrum, let her! Time passed quickly and the air was cooler. Calling the game to a halt, Lucy reached for a half dozen or so buttons which lay on the ground. Jacinta grabbed them first.

"Leave them alone, they're mine. I won them from you." She held the buttons tightly in her hands.

"Give them back at once," said the older girl," or I won't have time to sew them on, we've got to take the sheep out again."

"I can't help that, I won them and I want them to play with tomorrow."

"Oh come on, Jacinta," her brother broke in, "don't be so stubborn."

"Mind your own business," she yelled at him.

"J-A-C-I-N-T-A," Lucy said threateningly, "I'll never play with you again if you don't give them back *now*"

Realising this was the ultimatum she flung the offending items at her cousin. The episode went no further.

"What are you doing?" A reproving voice came from behind. The startled children turned. *"Pray, pray a great deal. The Most Holy Hearts of Jesus and Mary have plans for you, offer up prayers and sacrifices continually to the Almighty."*

It was the angel.

Plucking up courage Lucy swallowed and then asked, "How are we to make sacrifices?"

"In every way you can, offering them up as an act of reparation for the sins by which the Almighty is offended and for the conversion of sinners. By doing this you will draw peace upon your country, I am its guardian angel, the angel of Portugal. Above all," he continued, *"accept and endure all the suffering which God will send you."* With

this message imparted he disappeared as quickly as he had come.

The two girls were transfixed to the spot and so they would have remained had not Francisco nudged his cousin,

"What did he say then?"

"Why, didn't you listen?" exclaimed his astonished sister. "Of course I did. I heard what Lucy said, but like last time I didn't hear the angel even though I saw his lips move. Come on, tell me."

Lucy was quite overwhelmed, the experience had taken a lot out of her. "I'm not able to speak now....I'll tell you tomorrow.....or you can ask Jacinta." But she too was totally drained and motioned her brother to be quiet. Francisco somehow understood and, like his companions, thought about what had happened.

Over a period of days Francisco was told the message, but he was unable to understand its meaning; it fell to Lucy to explain as best she could.

The summer passed, and with the arrival of autumn shepherds once again spent all day out with their flocks. Although rather nippy, the weather was nevertheless pleasing and today the cousins unhurriedly led the sheep to pasture. While scuffing fallen leaves and kicking acorns and olives ahead of him Francisco occasionally burst into song. The two girls with hands joined skipped happily along beside him.

After passing Pregueira, a small olive grove belonging to the Santos family, they went around the hillside, clambering over very large rocks of the Cabeço before settling their sheep, and then, beside a little cave, prayed. They said the rosary, prostrated themselves and repeated the angel's prayer. A bright light made them look up. Before them standing on a rock was the angel.

In his hands he held a chalice into which fell drops of blood from a host above it. Leaving both suspended in mid air he stretched himself out on the ground beside the shepherds.

"Listen to this prayer carefully," he said, *"and repeat it after me three times: Most Holy Trinity, Father, Son and Holy Spirit, I offer you the most precious body and blood, soul and divinity of Jesus Christ present in all the tabernacles of the earth, in reparation for the outrages and indifferences with which He Himself is offended. And through the infinite merits of His Most Sacred Heart and of the Immaculate Heart of Mary, I beg of you the conversion of poor sinners."*

He stood up, took hold of the chalice and host, giving the latter to Lucy and the blood to Francisco and Jacinta, *"Take and drink the body and blood of Jesus Christ horribly insulted by ungrateful men. Make reparation for their sins and console your God."*

Prostrating once more their visitor had them say again the prayer to the Trinity, then he left.

After this apparition, though filled with considerable happiness, the children were physically exhausted and for some time were thoughtful and quiet, until Francisco, who of the three least understood, began questioning.

"I know the angel gave you communion, Lucy, but what about me and Jacinta?"

Jacinta it was who replied, "We received communion too....it's exactly the same...surely you saw the blood drip from the Host?"

The boy's eyes shone. "I felt Jesus was inside me because I was so happy but didn't understand how...now I know."

Enveloped by the sublimity of it all they continued praying. Later, on the way home, Jacinta spoke in an awed whisper, "What would your mother say, Lucy, if she knew Francisco and me had received communion? She told us at her catechism class we'd have to wait until we're ten."

"I dread to think," shuddered the girl, "just don't tell her, that's all, or anyone else, come to that."

To all outward appearances the children behaved normally and no one suspected that they spent long hours praying and discussing what the angel said. One thing however continued to elude them, they could not fathom the meaning of the words:

"ABOVE ALL ACCEPT THE SUFFERINGS THE LORD WILL SEND YOU".

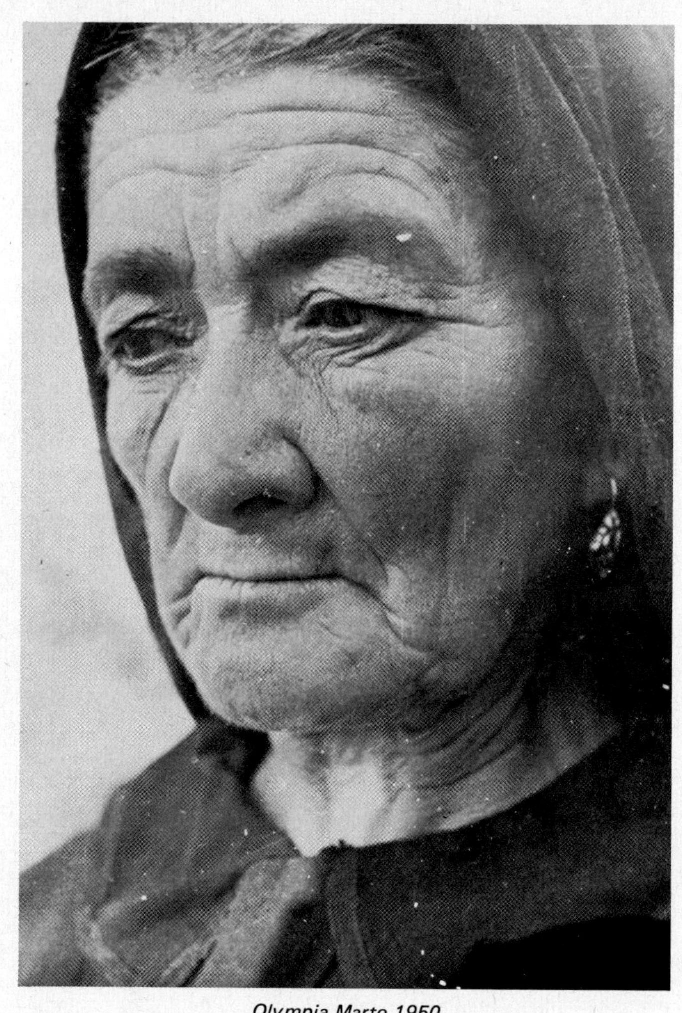

Olympia Marto 1950

CHAPTER FOUR

"WHAT DO YOU WANT OF US?"

Winter had come and gone and the Sierra D'Aire was at its most beautiful. April showers and a gentle warming sun had brought plants and trees magically to life; everywhere was ablaze with colour, flowers carpeting the earth and blossom laden trees.

Today, Sunday May 13th 1917, the three inseparable friends went slowly with their flock across the Sierra, letting them graze on the way.

At about noon they reached the Cova da Iria, a large natural hollow, part of which belonged to Lucy's parents. Skirting the cultivated land they stopped on the ascent at the far end, where the rock scattered land was fit only for grazing, and after chasing the sheep up the hill, sat down to eat lunch. Lucy's as usual was frugal. Since her cousins had become shepherds, however, she had fared very much better. Being more prosperous, the Marto children's packed lunches always contained a greater variety of food. How their cousin looked forward to sharing such delicacies as sweet cakes and succulent little sausages, so much a rarity in her own home, where it was always a day to day struggle to make ends meet.

When they had finished eating and prayed the rosary, Francisco suggested building a castle. While he prepared the site Lucy and Jacinta gathered some rocks. Engrossed in their project they were surprised by a sudden flash of light. Lucy's experienced eyes scanned the cloudless sky; it did not look stormy to her...but.....lightning meant only one thing.

"Come on," she scrambled to her feet, "we're in for bad weather, let's get home." The other two wasted no time and the sheep were quickly gathered and chased down the slope. They had not gone very far when another flash of light hastened them on. A few steps further the girls came to an abrupt halt in front of a tiny holm oak. Their mouths fell open as they beheld a lady dressed in white, her feet touching the top branches of the tree. She was ringed in a brilliant light which enveloped the children.

The Lady spoke: *"Don't be afraid, I won't hurt you."*

Lucy managed to find her voice, "Who are you? Where do you come from?"

"I am from heaven."

"What do you want of us?"

"I came to ask you to come here for six months in succession at the same hour. Then I will tell you who I am and what I want....afterwards I shall come a seventh time."

"Shall I go to heaven?" There was no sign of fear in Lucy's voice.

"Yes you will".

"And Jacinta?"

"Yes, she will go also."

"And Francisco?"

"Yes, but first he must say many rosaries".

Hearing his name mentioned, Francisco retraced his footsteps and looked at the girls in amazement, "Whatever are you doing talking to a tree?"

"Ssh...can't you see the Lady?"

"What lady? I can't see anything....here throw a stone....see if it's real."

Lucy was horrified; "Don't say such things!" Then to the Lady, "Francisco can't see you."

"Tell him to say a rosary so he will."

Lucy passed on the message and before the first decade came to an end he saw her. Jacinta tugged Lucy's arm, "D'you think the Lady's hungry? Ask her if she wants some bread and cheese."

Before her cousin could answer, Francisco whispered,

"What about the sheep? They've wandered off, they'll eat the peas."

"No they won't, don't worry, the Lady said they'll be alright." Now very much at ease Lucy remembered her two friends who had died recently. "Is Maria das Neves in heaven?"

"Yes, she is."

"And Amelia?"

"She will be in purgatory until the end of the world." Then she continued, *"Do you wish to offer yourselves to God, to endure all the sufferings he may send you as an act of reparation for the sins by which he is offended, and to ask for the conversion of sinners?"*

"Yes we do." Lucy answered for all three.

"Then you will have much to suffer but God will comfort you." As she spoke these words her hands opened for the first time, and from the palms came two streams of light so intense they penetrated the very being of the visionaries causing them instinctively to pray, "Oh Most Holy Trinity I adore you. My God I love you."

A few moments later the Lady added, *"Say the rosary every day to obtain peace for the world and an end to the war."* Almost at once she began to rise from the holm oak, serenly going up towards the East. The great light which surrounded her went on ahead as if carving out a passage through the skies. They stared until there was nothing more to see, then all was quiet. Francisco made the first move and ran off to see what mischief the sheep had been up to.

"Hey," he called from the vegetable patch, "not one pea's been nibbled!"

"I told you so," Lucy shouted back, "the Lady said they'd be alright."

"How was I to know," retorted Francisco," I didn't hear her speak."

It was a mystified little boy, who with his staff prodded

the woolly intruders back up the slope. Sitting down on some rocks Lucy explained to him all the Lady said, especially about the many rosaries he must say.

Time passed and they made tracks for home, quiet and thoughtful; the silence was broken from time to time by Jacinta who burst out, "Oh, what a beautiful lady."

Eventually Lucy warned, "We'd better not tell anybody or we'll get into trouble." Francisco nodded, Jacinta said nothing.

"Did you hear me, Jacinta?"

"Oh, what a beautiful lady," she said dreamily.

"Jacinta," Lucy shouted, "you must keep this a secret."

"Alright," Jacinta said automatically.

"I just know you'll end up telling someone. Promise me you won't say a word....not even to your mother."

Jerking herself to the present the little girl replied, "Of course I won't tell anyone....I promise".

Arriving back at Aljustrel they went to their respective homes and bedded the sheep; Lucy carried on as normal and said nothing about the remarkable event, likewise Francisco, Jacinta on the other hand stood anxiously by the door awaiting her parents' return from Batalha.

Eventually they came into sight. Olympia Marto, carrying a large bundle on her head, was a few strides in front of her husband who led a piglet bought at market. Jacinta rushed forward, "Mama, Mama," she threw her arms around the woman, "I saw Our Lady at the Cova today."

"My, my," she said, "fancy that, you must certainly be a very good little girl to see Our Lady."

"I did see her, Mama, I did see her," Jacinta jumped up and down, "so did Lucy and Francisco." Seeing the disbelief on her mother's face she went to her father who was putting away the piglet.

"I saw Our Lady today, Papa, so did...."

"Since when don't you give your father a kiss when you haven't seen him all day." He leaned towards her, she obliged. Hand in hand they went into the house, his daughter persisting with her story.

Knowing the girl did not tell lies, Senhora Marto decided to give the matter an airing during supper.

"Now Jacinta tell us again what happened at the Cova."

She needed no coaxing, "I saw a beautiful lady. She wore a long white dress and a cloak.....there was a golden cord round her neck....and some stars on her dress too." The child stopped, joined her hands together as if to pray, "She stood like this and held a shiny white rosary..." Jacinta's face was radiant. "Our Lady only spoke to Lucy, but she said we'd all go to heaven and lots of other things I didn't understand...but Lucy did.....after that she floated away and the doors opened in the sky and she went right into heaven!" The little girl paused for breath, then sighed, "Oh, what a beautiful lady!"

All was silent until her brother John started to giggle. Jacinta, upset, lowered her head, only to raise it again when Francisco re-echoed her story adding, "The Lady told Lucy she would come again every month for six months, and we've got to be there."

A pensive Manuel Marto fingered his moustache, then leaning forward in his chair said solemnly, "Well, who knows, it's possible. Not that many years ago Our Lady appeared to Bernadette at Lourdes....and before that to three other shepherds. All I know is that she comes when the world is in a bad way and it couldn't be worse now." He paused, "How are we to know? She may well have come to the Cova, but I think," he turned to his youngest, "that we should be quiet and leave everything in God's hands."

It did not take long, however, for the news to spread. When Maria-Rosa first heard she laughed, not for long though, as she realised her daughter was involved!

The first thing Francisco did in the morning was to inform Lucy of his sister's wagging tongue.

"I knew you'd tell, I just knew you would," Lucy reproached the culprit, "it happened just as I thought."

With that Jacinta burst into tears. "I couldn't help it....there was something inside me that stopped me from being quiet.

"Oh alright, stop crying, but don't tell anyone what the Lady told us."

"But I already did."

"Oh no, what did you say?"

"That the Lady promised to take us to heaven....forgive me, please forgive me...I won't ever tell anyone again."

Once in the pastures Jacinta sat on a rock, quiet and pensive. "Come and play," her cousin called.

"I don't want to play today."

"Why not?"

"Because I'm thinking how that lady told us to say the rosary and make many sacrifices for sinners...we'll have to say the 'Our Father' and 'Hail Mary' properly now."

It was Lucy's turn to be quiet on the way home. She felt worried, and not without cause.

"What's all this gossip going round the village?" was her mother's greeting.

"What do you mean, Mama?"

"Don't give me that, you know perfectly well what I mean...all this business about seeing something at the Cova."

"It's true, I did, and so did Francisco and Jacinta."

"Ah, I bet that little monkey put you up to it, come on now, I want to hear the whole load of lies from your own lips." After listening to the account she turned on her daughter, "You're a little liar, trying to stir up trouble with your pranks. Don't you dare let me hear another word of it." Then shaking her daughter, "D'you hear?"

Much to the chagrin of Maria-Rosa and other members of the Santos household the affair did not end there. Tongues started to wag and both parents and children met with ridicule. What annoyed her most was that people went to the Cova to pray.

One morning, as Lucy was leaving with the sheep, Maria-Rosa's rage got the better of her.

"D'you know you're bringing us disgrace? We used to be the most respected family in Aljustrel," she screamed. "Now look at us, we're a laughing stock....stop this stubbornness, girl, and confess you lied."

"Oh, Mama, please believe me...you know I never tell lies."

"Well, you're lying now." Her face red with fury the woman took hold of the yardbroom and beat her petrified daughter. "Tonight, my girl, I'm taking you to all the people you've deceived, then you'll own up to your lies!"

Waiting at the Barreiro pond Francisco and Jacinta could hear their cousin sobbing as she approached with the sheep.

"What's the matter?" They ran to meet her.

Lucy explained and then asked: "What can I do? Mama wants me to say I'm telling lies and if I do, that'll be a lie!"

Francisco was very upset at his cousin's anguish, "It's all your fault," he said to Jacinta, "why did you have to tell them?"

The latter began to cry and knelt before Lucy begging forgiveness, "I did wrong, I'll never tell again."

"Forget it now," she embraced the youngster. "Let's get going."

Although the elder girl put on a brave face, she could not rid her mind of the evening encounter with her mother. Fortunately for Lucy, Maria-Rosa did not carry out her threat that evening. She had talked with Olympia during the day, and although her sister-in-law did not entirely share her husband's views, she was nevertheless able to reassure Maria-Rosa somewhat.

"You don't really think those rascals will go to the Cova on June 13th, do you? It's the feast of St. Anthony...can you imagine them missing all the fun?"

"No, I suppose you're right," the woman relaxed a little, "my Lucy adores dancing . . . and all that extra food!"

"There you are then," Olympia smiled, "there's nothing to worry about, you'll see, this thing will fizzle out in no time!"

CHAPTER FIVE

SAINT ANTHONY'S DAY

It was the morning of June 13th, the feast of St. Anthony, patron saint of Fatima, and Senhora Santos felt a great sense of relief as she made her way to Mass. Lucy had returned from the pastures, changed into her best clothes and gone on ahead.

Fatima in honour of St. Anthony was well decorated, and when Maria-Rosa arrived people were milling around everywhere. The village band played and bells rang out joyfully; tables laden with food stood ready for eating, and ox-carts filled with fresh home baked bread to be blessed and distributed, stood outside the church door. Nevertheless the woman battled through and managed to get a seat at the front.

After Mass, while mingling with other members of the congregation, her son sought her out.

"Mama, Lucy's just gone down the road with some other girls. They went as soon as Mass was over." He could hardly get the words out quickly enough, "I tried to stop her...." His voice trailed off.

Maria-Rosa flushed angrily. "That stupid girl....I bet she's going to the Cova...she'll be sorry...and fancy making those girls miss the procession and lovely food. She's a real hussy these days....I don't know what's come over her."

Meanwhile Lucy returned home with a few friends plus some men and women who had also decided to forgo the feast. At about eleven o'clock she called for her cousins, then followed by the others went to the Cova da Iria. Sitting near the holm oak the children amused themselves. Concerned that they were not bothering, some onlookers asked, "When's Our Lady coming?"

"Don't worry, she won't be long now," they were told.

The sun neared its zenith; Lucy stopped playing and became apprehensive. "We must say the rosary....it's almost

Mary's Immaculate Heart

time." They had hardly finished when the first flash came, followed by a slowly approaching bright light.

"Quickly," she ordered, and together with her two cousins hastened to the holm oak. They saw the Lady above the tree immediately, just as she was in May. Their friends who knelt a little apart did their best to hear though they saw nothing.

"Senhora, what do you want of me?"

"I want you to come here on the thirteenth day of the coming month, to recite the rosary every day and after each decade add, 'Oh Jesus forgive us our sins, save us from the fires of hell; lead all souls to heaven especially those in most need.' I want you to learn to read. Later I will tell you what else I want."

Lucy then asked for a favour; that a sick person she knew might be cured.

"If he is converted he will be cured during the year."

"I should like to ask you to take us to heaven."

"Yes, Jacinta and Francisco I will take soon, but you must remain here some time longer. Jesus wishes to make use of your services to make me known and loved. He wishes to have devotion to My Immaculate Heart established in the world."

"Have I got to stay here by myself?" Lucy was sad at the thought of her two cousins going without her.

"No, daughter. Do you suffer a great deal? Don't be discouraged....I'll never forsake you. My Immaculate Heart will be your refuge and the means that will lead you to God."

With these words the Lady opened her hands; an intense light permeated them. In it they could see themselves; Jacinta and Francisco were in the rays ascending to heaven while Lucy was in those spreading over the earth. Before the palm of the Lady's right hand was a heart encircled by thorns. This the children understood to be Mary's Immaculate Heart injured by sins.

The vision ended. Lucy cried out, "It's all over... look, there she goes." Eyes turned in the direction of a small white cloud which floated away until out of sight.

"That's it," Lucy said matter of factly, "she's gone into heaven...the doors have closed up."

The group of people surged forward excitedly; the holm oak's top branches were slightly bent as if someone had been standing on them. As one they pounced, picking leaves and breaking twigs for souvenirs, stopping only at Lucy's request; then they returned to Fatima, saying the rosary while walking.

Festivities were in full swing, but even so their arrival did not go unnoticed; questions were fired at them from all angles; the visionaries, however, told only what they felt able.

Francisco as before did not hear the Lady speak, also he could not work out what the rays of light represented; Lucy told him everything, explaining at the same time that he and Jacinta would soon go to heaven while she was to remain on earth for some time.

At home a little later the brothers and sisters of the youngest seers bombarded them with questions, but to no avail, Jacinta spoke only of the beauty of her Lady. They were in the parlour looking at and comparing pictures of Our Lady to see if they bore resemblance to the visitor, when their parents returned from market, having discretely absented themselves from the day's proceedings. Now they were surprised and not a little subdued on hearing the news.

"Well, what did she say this time?" Olympia demanded.

Jacinta lowered her head. "She said we must say the rosary and she's coming back again on the thirteenth of next month....she told us a secret too."

"What sort of secret?"

Jacinta bit her lip. "I can't tell you." And neither would she or Francisco, in spite of the bribes from all except their father, who soon silenced the uproar.

When Lucy's sisters heard there was a secret, not only did they offer bribes, but furious with her silence, threatened to punish her. Lucy's mother kept aloof throughout the rumpus until her youngest daughter went to bed, then she shouted, "If you don't put the people right by confessing you lied, I'll lock you up in a room where you won't even see the sunlight."

The frightened girl hid beneath the blankets; *What's happened to my family?* She thought, *they used to love me so much.*

Fireworks crackling in the distance brought this feast day to an end, and as they did so, Lucy lowered her lids over tear-filled eyes.

Lucy's Home as viewed from the Well

CHAPTER SIX

"YOU SAW HELL WHERE THE SOULS OF POOR SINNERS GO"

Lucy woke screaming; the nightmare was so vivid that she could recall every detail. The devil had been laughing at having deceived her and struggled to drive her into hell. Seeing herself in his claws she called for Our Lady to help, but it was her mother who came hurrying to find out the trouble. Her daughter's vague answer seemed satisfactory and so she returned to bed.

This was the culmination of days of doubt and torment following an interview by Father Ferreira, who hearing of the goings on, summoned Senhora Santos and her daughter to his presbytery.

Before being admitted Maria-Rosa said harshly to the trembling child, "Don't annoy me any more, tell the Padre you lied, d'you hear? Then on Sunday he can say in church it's lies, and that'll be the end of the whole thing."

Contrary to Lucy's expectations Father Ferreira's questions were put quietly and kindly; only when dismissing them did he issue this warning:

"Usually when such things happen, Our Lord tells these people to go and tell their spiritual directors everything, even sends a message, but you, you hide as much as you can. 'Say the rosary every day' is as much as I get from you; we do that anyway. Now look here, you be very careful, it's quite possible y'know, that this is a trick of the devil....anyway, go now, the future will tell us."

These final words impinged themselves indelibly on Lucy's mind, and with the unending mockery, coupled with malice from villagers and family alike, her depression deepened. She doubted the apparitions, lost all inclination for making sacrifices and was even on the point of confessing she lied. Her only source of comfort was her cousins, who remarkably for ones so young did their best to dispel her scruples.

"You mustn't confess you lied, because that would be a lie and to lie is sinful." said Francisco.

"Oh Lucy, it's not the devil," Jacinta insisted, he's so ugly and lives under the ground in hell. That lady is so beautiful, and we saw her go into heaven."

Nevertheless her doubts persisted, and on the eve of July 13th Lucy told the two quite firmly she had no intention of going to the Cova.

"If the Lady asks for me, tell her I'm not going because I'm afraid she is the devil."

By morning her attitude had not changed, but as the hour drew nearer she suddenly felt compelled to keep the appointment. Hastening to the Martos' home she found Jacinta kneeling at the foot of the bed crying her eyes out; Francisco stood beside her.

"Well, aren't you going then?"

"Without you we dare not," she sobbed.

"C'mon, I've changed my mind." Tears were quickly wiped away and the three set off: their journey was not easy, for along the route pilgrims waited, to beseech favours.

Following a short distance behind was Manuel Marto, ready to intervene if anything untoward happened, while his wife and Senhora Santos went to the Cova unnoticed and hid behind a bush.

On arrival at their destination the three seers knelt, Lucy just in front. She began the rosary and those gathered joined in. The sun blazed down unrelentlessly, and many held raised umbrellas as a protection. A flash of light rent the air, "She's coming; quickly, close the umbrellas," Lucy cried out. The sun lost its glare and there was a gentle cooling breeze; apart from a soft buzzing above the holm oak, all was silent.

Then Lucy spoke.

"Senhora, what do you want of me?"

"I want you to come here on the thirteenth day of next month and to keep saying the rosary every day in honour of Our Lady of the Rosary, to obtain peace for the world and the end of war, for she alone can help.

Remembering her mother's hostility and the Parish Priest's words, Lucy pleaded, "Please will you tell us who you are and perform a miracle so that everyone will believe you appeared to us?"

"Continue to come here every month. In October I will tell you who I am and what I wish, and I will perform a miracle so that people may believe," Then the Lady continued, *"It is necessary to pray the rosary to obtain graces during the year and, sacrifice yourselves for sinners and say many times, especially when you make a sacrifice: Jesus it is for love of you, for the conversion of sinners and in reparation for sins committed against the Immaculate Heart of Mary."*

When the Lady spoke these words she opened her hands as she had in the previous two months. The radiance seemed to penetrate the ground and the children saw a giant sea of fire. Plunged in it were demons and human beings looking as if they were red hot coals, transparent and black or bronze-coloured. They floated about amid clouds of smoke, without weight or equilibrium, shrieking and groaning in despair. The devils were distinguishable in the horrible loathsome forms of unknown animals.

The children were horrified and raised their eyes appealingly to the Lady. With tenderness and sadness she said, *"You saw hell where the souls of poor sinners go. To save them God wants to establish in the world devotion to My Immaculate Heart. If they do what I tell you many souls will be saved and there will be peace. The war is going to end. But if they do not stop offending God another, even worse, will begin in the reign of Pius XI. When you see a night illuminated by an unknown light, know that this is the great sign God gives you that he is going to punish the world for its crimes by means of war, hunger and persecutions of the Church and of the Holy Father. To prevent this I will come to ask for the consecration of Russia to My Immaculate Heart and the communion of reparation on the first Saturdays. If they listen to my requests Russia will be converted and there will be peace. If not she will scatter her errors throughtout the world, provoking wars and persecutions of the Church. The good will be martyred, the Holy Father will have much to suffer and various nations will be annihilated. In the end My Immaculate Heart will triumph. The Holy Father will consecrate Russia to me and it will be converted and a certain period of peace granted to the world. In Portugal the faith will always be kept. Tell this to no one. Francisco, yes, you may tell him. When you say the rosary say after each mystery, 'Oh Jesus, forgive us our sins, save us from the fires of hell, lead all souls to heaven especially those in most need.'"*

A short period of silence followed before Lucy asked, "Do you want anything else of me?"

"No, today I desire nothing more."

The visitation ended, and as usual, the Lady began to rise towards the East.

"Lucy, Lucy, what happened? You all looked so sad." The crowd converged on the children. Their mothers, peering from behind the bush, were concerned for their offspring; this turned to relief on seeing Jacinta in the arms of her father, while Lucy and Francisco were being carried by two tall men. Though many followed, others stayed behind to pray and leave money.

As days went by, it became increasingly more difficult for the visionaries to avoid those who sought them out. Both houses were harrassed by visitors: peace was to be found only in the fields.

Since the first apparition the youngsters had lost all interest in dancing and games, particularly Jacinta;

"I don't want to play; that lady told us to make

sacrifices, how are we to do that?"

"I know," Francisco had an idea, "we'll give our lunch to the sheep today." This they did and continued doing until one day some beggar children passed them.

"Quickly," Jacinta said, "lets have the lunches. I'll give them to those poor children."

Ever after this the beggars waited around to collect their daily supply. Needless to say by mid-afternoon each day the three shepherds were extremely hungry, so they ate flowers and pine tree roots. Jacinta, not sure whether this was a sufficient sacrifice, chose to eat bitter acorns and unripe olives. When Lucy told her not to eat them because they were bitter, she replied, "Oh, it's because they are that I eat them, to convert sinners."

With the advent of hot weather they returned home for lunch and spent siesta time at the Santos well. One afternoon Jacinta remained sitting beside it while the other two went off to look for wild honey.

"Did you see the Holy Father?" she asked when they returned.

"No."

"I don't know how it happened, but I saw the Holy Father in a very big house, kneeling by a table with his hands on his face, and he was weeping. Outside the house there were many people; some of them were throwing stones at him, others were cursing and saying ugly words."

It was the first of other visions in which Jacinta saw the Pope. Another time she said:

"Can't you see all those highways and roads and fields full of people weeping and starving for want of food? And the Holy Father in a church praying before the Immaculate Heart of Mary? And many people praying with him? Poor Holy Father, we must pray much for him."

This they proceeded to do, but it was the vision of hell and lost souls that caused most concern, driving them in search of sacrifices.

July being so hot presented a golden opportunity; the cousins decided to forgo drinking until returning home at siesta time. One day in particular a rich pasturage was offered them, but it was some distance from Aljustrel; this meant staying out all day. The heat was unbearable, and by mid-afternoon, having had neither food nor drink, they felt really ill. Anxious for the well-being of her cousins Lucy went to the nearest house for water. Returning she handed Francisco a jug of cool clear liquid.

"No," he pushed it away, "I don't want to drink.... I want to suffer for sinners that they might change their ways."

"Here Jacinta, you drink."

"No, I want to suffer too."

Lucy poured the water into a hollow, where it was soon lapped up by thirsty sheep. As the heat intensified, lack of fluid began to take its toll on Jacinta. "Tell the crickets and frogs to be quiet, I have a terrible headache." She covered her ears.

"Don't you want to offer it up for sinners?" said Francisco.

Lowering her hands the little mite whispered "Yes...yes I do...let them sing. Oh Lucy, why doesn't Our Lady show hell to sinners? If they saw it they wouldn't sin any more."

Whereas Francisco and his sister had to seek suffering, Lucy was never long without it. Her family became daily more vicious, especially after losing their vegetables at the Cova. "When you want to eat, girl, you ask Our Lady for yours," scolded her parents, "and," her sisters tormented, "you should only eat the weeds growing in the Cova."

As more people came to the village and Cova da Iria Maria-Rosa's worries increased. Someone always had something to say:

"Well, Senhora, what do you make of your daughter's visions?"

"I don't know." The woman wrung her hands. "I think she is a liar and has half the world deceived."

"Don't say that," he sneered, "or someone is liable to kill her."

"I don't care about that so long as they make her confess the truth. I will tell the truth even if it means condemning my children...or myself, come to that."

The day following this particular episode, Maria-Rosa took her daughter to the Parish Priest in another effort to drag out a confession.

On the way she kept up a non-stop sermon until Lucy, frightened by her mother's anger, cried out,

"Mama, how can I say I didn't see when I did?"

At this outburst her mother became silent until at the presbytery door she said fiercely, "All I want you to do is to tell the truth. If you saw, say so, if you didn't then confess, but, my girl, you'd better be sure."

During the meeting Fr. Ferreira questioned Lucy, doing his best to trick and confuse her, but his efforts were fruitless. Shrugging his shoulders he dismissed the pair.

Back at the well, her cousins, who knew where Lucy had gone, waited anxiously.

When she arrived, eyes brimming with tears, Jacinta cried too and cuddling the unhappy girl said, "Oh Lucy, I do so wish my family were like yours and treated me bad, then I'd have more sacrifices to offer Our Lord."

Manuel Marto 1956

CHAPTER SEVEN

THE SUMMONS

Lucy returned from the fields at midday, put the sheep in their pen and went into the kitchen. She was very hot and wanted only to have a wash and a cool down. Before she could do so, however, her father thrust a piece of paper forward.

"See this? It's an official summons from the administrator of Ourem...he wants to see you tomorrow."

"What for, Papa?"

"Here, read it to her." Antonio Santos thrust the paper at his wife. Wiping her hands dry she took the letter, glared at her daughter and began:

"...you are hereby ordered with your child to appear before a special meeting with His Excellency, the Administrator of Vila Nova de Ourem, and the aforementioned child to give good reason for disturbing the peace. Said trial is to be held at 12 noon on August 11th 1917."

By order of:
His Excellency Artur Oliviera Santos,
Adminstrator of Vila Nova de Ourem

"You see, Lucy, you see what your lies have done," Antonio shouted. "Now we're in trouble. The Administrator is a very important man, he can do anything to you, even put you to death...for goodness sake confess before it's too late."

"You stubborn girl," her mother stormed, "why don't you give in?"

"But, Mama, I keep telling you, how can I say I didn't see the Lady when I did?"

Her father, at a loss for words and fearing he might strike the girl, went to confer with his brother-in-law, who had also been summoned.

"Well," Manuel Marto said, "I'm going but I'm not taking the children. If that pompous fool thinks I'm taking my youngsters on a nine mile hike he's got another think coming."

"Well, my girl's going, she's got us into this mess, so let her answer for it, if she's lying then she deserves to be punished."

The next day at dawn, Lucy was put astride a donkey, and, led by her father, they went to call for Senhor Marto. He was not quite ready, which gave Lucy an opportunity to see her companions.

Jacinta still in bed welcomed her visitor with open arms. "If they kill you," she said earnestly, "tell them Francisco and me want to die too."

Hearing her father call, the elder girl broke away, "Oh, Jacinta, I feel so unhappy." Blowing her cousin a kiss she left the room.

Jacinta called after her:

"Francisco and me'll go to the well and pray for you; if you come back, meet us there."

The journey for Lucy was tiring; three times she fell from the donkey and at Ourem she could hardly stand because of aching limbs. The party were immediately shown into the magistrate's office, where Artur Oliviera Santos sat arrogantly behind his desk. There were no preliminaries; his clerks sat with pens poised ready to write down every detail; the interrogation was on. After a few questions he suddenly shot out, "Where are the other children?"

Senhor Marto spoke up, "They're at home."

"What are they doing there? I ordered you to bring them."

"They're far too young to appear before a magistrate's court, besides, it's a long way from our village. They can't even ride a donkey yet."

"That's not my problem, it was up to you to get them here. When I give an order I expect it to be obeyed." He pointed a finger at Lucy, "Now you, let's see what you've got to say for yourself...what d'you mean causing all this trouble? Dreaming up an imaginary lady...eh...eh!" He leaned towards her, "and all this rubbish about flashes of light and cosy talks. Look at all the good folk you're deceiving with your play acting; your little game's turned into something big now, hasn't it? Encouraging people to pray to a tree!" He paused for breath, "Say something, young miss, have you lost your tongue?"

Lucy hung her head, "It was a real lady, Senhor, the three of us saw her, and she spoke."

"What did she say?"

"She told us to say the rosary every day."

"What else...come now, there's talk of a secret?"

"I can't tell you, Senhor."

"What d'you mean can't? Won't is more like it."

"If I told you, it wouldn't be a secret any more...would it?" Lucy said innocently.

The young man became more angry, "Don't you dare speak to me like that...I can *make* you tell me, you know that surely?"

Lucy said nothing, her father shifted uneasily on his feet.

"You've got to tell me the secret."

The child remained silent.

"I can quite easily have you killed!"

Unable to break through he changed his tactics. "Come along now, there's a good girl, tell me the secret and I'll forget all about how naughty you've been, you won't be punished."

There was no answer despite a prod from her father. The magistrate then turned towards him, "You, what do the people of Fatima think of this?"

"Oh...er...nothing, Your Excellency. They say it's woman's gossip."

The administrator looked questioningly at Manuel Marto, who stood calmly before him.

"I agree with my children."

"You believe it's true?"

"Yes, Senhor, I believe it's true, my children never tell lies."

The administrator's guffaw echoed round the sparsely furnished room, causing supercilious grins to landscape the faces of his minions. Scowling again he turned on Lucy, "Promise me you won't go to this Cova place again.

Antonio pushed his daughter, "Lucy, tell His Excellency you'll do as he says."

"Is the girl an idiot, why doesn't she answer?" Then raising his voice, "I forbid you to go any more, d'you hear?"

"Your Excellency," Antonio fidgeted nervously with the hat he held, "she won't cause you any more trouble, I'll see to it."

Banging his fist on the desk the administrator continued, "Make sure you *do* see to it, I've wasted enough time as it is, now get out before I lock you all up."

A clerk opened the door and ushered them out. Artur Santos watched their departure from his open window, and his face contorted with anger on noticing a file of people, mostly women, going in the direction of Fatima.

"You're mad," he bellowed, "listening to the prattlings of children, you ought to be in your fields working, not going on a fool's errand." Nodding towards three of his henchmen, he snapped, "Get to Aljustrel, interview those children and find out everything you can. I'm going to put an end to this business for good."

CHAPTER EIGHT

"THE SECRET...THE SECRET!"

The thirteenth of August dawned; since the previous day pilgrims had converged on Aljustrel. They all wanted to see the children, question them and ask for petitions to be put to the Lady. Lucy was in the middle of one such buffeting, with voices coming at her from all directions, when she was ordered to go at once with her father to the Marto house. Awaiting them was Artur Oliviera Santos. Lucy flinched at seeing her interrogator again, but bravely stood beside Francisco and Jacinta who were with him.

"Ah," he smiled, "now I have the three of you together, you can tell me what happened at the Cova da Iria."

They told him.

"And what about the secret, surely you can tell me?" The cousins looked at the floor.

"Come along now, I won't tell anyone."

All was still. The smile left his face. "You've got to tell me, and promise not to go to the Cova again."

"Getting nowhere he called their fathers. "These brats of yours refuse to answer me. I want you to take them to the presbytery at once,"

The unexpected party surprised the Parish Priest; nevertheless, at the administrator's instigation, he cross-examined the seers. Time passed, and fearing they would miss their appointment the visionaries became agitated. With the roads to the Cova already overflowing with pilgrims, they knew their journey would take longer than usual.

"Come", said the administrator pleasantly, "I'll take you to the Cova myself, so you won't be late at all...my carriage is waiting at the presbytery steps."

The little ones declined the offer, but Lucy's father beckoned his daughter forward, "Go along into the carriage

Parish Church, Fatima

quickly." Having no option she did so, followed by the other seers.

They were driven in great haste across the church square towards the Cova da Iria, but suddenly the man cracked his whip, changed direction and made for Ourem.

"This isn't the way, Senhor", Lucy cried out, "you've taken the wrong road."

"Senhor, Senhor," Francisco tugged at their captor's sleeve.

"Be quiet all of you," and taking one hand from the reigns he tossed over a blanket, "Cover yourselves with this, heads as well, I don't want these people to see you."

Before Jacinta's fair head disappeared beneath the smelly cloth, she looked back helplessly, "Oh, why don't they come after us?" The little one could not understand it.

On arrival at Ourem Artur Santos went directly to his house and locked them in a room where they remained, except for periodic questioning; his kindly wife supplied some food. During the time alone they prayed, but as evening approached the interruptions became more frequent; always it was for the same reason, "Tell me the secret...the secret...the secret!"

On top of this they felt distressed at not having been to the Cova. Francisco tried lifting their spirits.

"Perhaps the Lady will come to us here instead." But when at the end of the day she failed to do so, he said despondently, "I so much want to see her again."

"Oh, Francisco, of course you'll see her again...even if we're killed we'll see her in heaven," Jacinta replied.

Night passed and the third degree continued. At mid-morning, having drawn a blank, the Administrator transferred them to the Court House, where an elderly woman asked more questions, doing her best to win their confidence and extract the secret. When this failed they were bribed with large sums of money, then threatened with death; all to no avail. Angered at so much obstinancy their captor had them taken back to his house.

The children were over the initial shock when in the afternoon questioning was resumed.

"Now, come on, enough of these games," Artur Santos put on a false smile, "you've kept it up long enough, tell me the secret and let's be done with it."

"No, we can't," Lucy was the spokesman, "the Lady told us not to tell anyone."

"Tell me, then I promise to let you play with my children out there in the sunshine...."

The seers looked at the pattern the sun made on the floor but said nothing.

"Tell me your secret," his voice rose, "or I'll have you killed in a horrible way."

No answer.

"Tell me, or I'll throw you in gaol!"

True to his word he did just that, but not before a final inquisition in his office. As he went over the same ground again and again, they stood silently before him and prayed.

"That's it...I've had enough, I've tried to be kind to you to make you see sense, but you haven't even the manners to answer me, to gaol with you. I'm going to have you boiled in oil!"

They were led from his office across the main hall. A heavy wood door was unlocked and they were pushed into the cell. It was quite large with rough walls and stone floor; two heavily barred windows looked into the street. The only furniture consisted of a few bunk beds, wooden benches, and in a corner, overflowing buckets.

The stench was nauseating; stale sweat, unwashed bodies and unemptied buckets, coupled with overcrowding and the heat of the day.

As the door closed behind them Jacinta began crying;

"I want my Mama...Oh, why don't our parents come? We're going to die without seeing them." The tears streamed down her face. Lucy and Francisco, who had the same thoughts, sadly shook their heads.

"Don't cry," Francisco's arms went round his sister, let's offer it up as a sacrifice for poor sinners."

The seven year old joined her hands and all three said quietly, *"Oh my Jesus, it is for love of you, for the conversion of sinners and in reparation for sins committed against the Immaculate Heart of Mary."*

"And," added Jacinta, "for the Holy Father."

Thieves, murderers, drunkards, some staring vacantly, stayed put on benches, or huddled on the filth of the floor. Others surged forward to peer curiously at the new intake.

"Well, well, well, what have we here, babes in arms? They're starting very early these days!"

"What are you doing here?" A tough looking character, who seemed to be the leader, asked roughly.

"Oh, Senhor," Lucy cried out, "we're going to be killed because we won't tell the secret."

"Secret...what secret?"

"The Lady who visits us said we must tell no one."

"Ah," a voice came from behind, "these must be the seers of Fatima we've heard so much about." Jacinta's tears began to flow again, "I don't mind dying," she sobbed, "because Our Lady will come for me, but I just want to see Mama first."

"Why don't you tell that pig what he wants to know and get out of here?" This came from the spokesman.

"Oh, no, Senhor," the eldest replied, "we'd rather die."

Seeing no let up in the children's distress, one of the prisoners' played a small concertina and the others sang. Trying further to cheer up the babes, it was suggested they dance. Three of the men took a child each and whirled around; Jacinta being so tiny had to be carried in the arms of her partner. Suddenly she remembered her Lady.

"Please, please put me down, I don't want to dance." Standing once more she took from around her neck a medal and had the man hang it from a nail in the wall, then she knelt. Lucy and Francisco left their partners and joined her, where oblivious to all they began to say the rosary. On and on they chanted, remembering to add the extra prayer at the end of each decade.

Gradually voices lowered and the music became softer until it stopped altogether. Heads turned towards the kneeling figures, some felt embarrasment and turned quickly away, but into many others came an awareness. Knees unaccustomed to kneeling creaked as they met the stone floor, lips which knew nothing but blasphemy stumbled over long forgotten prayers; the murmur grew until almost all were praying.

While this was going on, Francisco noticed a prisoner wearing his hat.

"Excuse me, Senhor, it's disrespectful to pray with your hat on". The man reddened, dropping it on the floor. Francisco politely picked up the offending item and gently placed it on a bench.

Later that afternoon the heavy door swung open to admit a guard.

"It's time now," he leered, "the oil is ready for you, we've had it boiling for over an hour." He grabbed Jacinta by the arm and led her from the cell. Though convinced death awaited her the little mite made no protest.

"Oh, Lucy," Francisco smiled at his cousin, they're going to kill us now, that means we'll be in heaven soon, won't that be wonderful? We're so lucky." Lucy nodded as he continued, "I do hope Jacinta's not frightened, let's say a 'Hail Mary' for her."

His sister meanwhile was being bombarded with

questions which she met with silence.

"Talk...talk! damn you...!" The administrator's face was ugly and twisted, the girl remained serene as she prayed.

"Take her away," he shouted at the guard. Francisco was next, but he too refused to save his skin by telling the secret. Lucy's turn came and as the cell door closed behind her, there was hardly a dry eye among those who remained.

In the office she related the visions but Artur Santos was not interested, he had a fixation, "The secret", he said, "the secret!"

"I can't tell you, Senhor, the Lady told us not to."

Once again in the hands of the guard she was marched off, praying as she went for courage to face death as bravely as the other two. A door opened and she was flung into the room. "Lucy, Lucy," Francisco and Jacinta ran towards her, "you're alive!"

Some time later, with the secret still intact, they were taken to the Administrator's house. At ten o'clock the next morning the procedure was as before: transferred to the Court House and tormented with questions. Finally their persecutor was forced to admit defeat, and fearing reprisals if he kept the children any longer, drove them back to the presbytery at Fatima from where he had abducted them.

Hoping for a quick getaway he reckoned without the crowds coming from Mass on this Assumption day. They recognised him and, already smouldering with anger, began to close in. Shouting broke out and a group of youths armed with sticks moved forward menacingly. Manuel Marto forseeing the consequences, grabbed the children and ran up to the presbytery balcony. He showed the unharmed youngsters to the mob in an endeavour to calm them. The Parish Priest, hearing this commotion, came out of church to find its cause. Seeing various persons on his balcony he hastened up the steps and wrongfully accused Manuel of causing a disturbance. On learning the facts, he suggested that in order to avoid local government trouble, the magistrate be escorted from Fatima.

Despite feeling repugnance for this man, Manuel Marto did just that and saw him safely on the road to Vila Nova de Ourem.

CHAPTER NINE

A VERY UNUSUAL PERFUME

The crowds waiting at the Cova da Iria on August 13th were fidgety and anxious at the non-arrival of the seers, and when at almost midday news came of the kidnapping, they nearly went mad. Had it not been for a sudden flash of light, the majority would have invaded the presbytery demanding Fr. Ferreira to obtain the children's release.

Fast on the heels of the flash came a clap of thunder. Above the holm oak a small white cloud hovered, while faces and clothing of pilgrims glowed with a variation of colour: red, pink, blue, green, yellow. From the sky fell a shower similar to snowflakes which settled for a while on nearby trees, giving them the impression of being in full bloom.

The overwhelmed spectators reached out with arms and umbrellas in an endeavour to catch some, but as they did so it just vanished. Finally the cloud lifted from the holm oak and sailed away to the East. Everyone who witnessed these signs felt sure that Our Lady, in spite of the children's absence, had kept her appointment and they went away happier.

Not so the parents of Francisco and Jacinta; when evening came with no sign of their youngsters, Olympia sought out her sister-in-law.

"What shall we do?" She held her aching head, "they'll probably be killed."

Down to earth Maria-Rosa knew that this would not be the case, and furthermore she did not particularly mind what they did to Lucy so long as her girl owned up. Therefore, when on the fifteenth of August the children came home, Lucy's return was celebrated by being told to go out immediately with the flock.

Her aunt and uncle were so happy at having their two

youngest returned safe and sound that they kept them in, cared for and cleaned them of filth, listened with horror to their experiences and lavished them with love. John, their brother, was sent out with the sheep.

Life returned to normal and the young shepherds resumed their duties. On Sunday the 19th, having lunched at the house of some friends in the village of Moita, it was necessary to return home and take out the flocks. Olympia, deciding to keep Jacinta in, made John go in her stead. As time was getting on, they went to nearby Valinhos.

Quite unexpectedly the light dimmed and the air became cooler; Lucy sensed that something was about to happen.

"D'you feel anything, Francisco?"

"Yes I do. Perhaps Our Lady's coming today as we weren't at the Cova on the 13th. Oh dear, what about Jacinta? It'll be a pity if she misses out."

"John," Lucy turned to her cousin, "please will you go and get Jacinta? She'll be sad if she misses her Lady."

"No, I'm not going," John retorted, "I want to see her too."

"Oh please," Francisco pleaded with his brother. "Look, if you run, you'll both be back in time."

He would not budge. Becoming agitated at a flash of light, Lucy pushed two coins into his hands.

"Here, take these, there'll be two more when you get back."

John needed no further persuading, and in a short space of time returned with his sister. Hardly had they all sunk to their knees when the Lady showed herself, as always, above a small tree.

"What do you want of me, Senhora?"

"I want you to continue going to the Cova da Iria on the thirteenth day of the month and to keep saying the rosary every day."

Lucy then told of how many disbelieved, and asked for

Valinhos Today

a miracle that everyone would know they told the truth.

"In October I shall perform a miracle so that all may believe."

"What do you want done with the money people leave at the Cova?" was Lucy's next question.

"Let them make two portable biers. Carry one with Jacinta and two other girls; you must all be dressed in white. Francisco is to carry the other one with three boys; they too must wear white. The money placed on these stands is for Our Lady of the Rosary's feast day, and any left over is to go towards the chapel which is going to be built."

Lucy then spoke of the many intentions she had been asked, especially for the sick.

"Yes, I will cure some within the year," was the answer. And then very sadly, *"Pray, pray a great deal, and make sacrifices for sinners. So many souls go to hell because they have no one to sacrifice and pray for them."*

With these her final words on this day she began to rise, going slowly away. The three seers came out of their trance overjoyed; poor John on the other hand, astonished with the goings on, had stared and listened, yet neither saw nor heard.

With the apparition over, Francisco reminded his sister that she was not looking after the sheep, so must go home. She did, but not before picking branches from the tree to keep as souvenirs.

Armed with hers, Jacinta stopped off at her aunt's to break the news; Maria-Rosa's feelings were unchanged.

"Oh, you wretches, you're up to your tricks again. I'd have thought the administrator would have knocked all that nonsense out of your heads."

Jacinta looked crest-fallen, "But, Aunt, that lady did come to see us just now, honestly; look, here's the branch she stood on."

Taking it from the child she examined it, sniffed, frowned, sniffed again. “This is very unusual perfume....what is it?” Then, handing the branch to the others present, “What d’you make of it? It’s only a piece of holm oak, yet the smell is beautiful.” They were all amazed at the sweet fragrance but none could put a name to it.

Retrieving her treasured possession, Jacinta hurried home to show her father. He was late coming in and although the perfume had faded he never doubted that the Lady had once more appeared.

The children with early believers at the site of apparitions, Cova da Iria

CHAPTER TEN

"DOES SHE SMILE?"

During the weeks which followed, others with anti-Catholic sympathies joined Artur Santos in his attempts to discredit the Fatima apparitions. Abusive articles were printed and leaflets decrying them as some Jesuitical hoax were distributed. Meetings inciting the public to action were arranged and one such was planned to take place outside the Fatima church after Sunday Mass. The plan back-fired when Father Ferreira got to hear of it and went elsewhere. Not to be outdone, a certain gentleman tried his best at the Cova, but he was ridiculed and his speech remained undelivered. Reporters too pestered the Marto and Santos households, using wile and cunning to expose them as imposters.

Meanwhile the children, unperturbed by these events, continued their daily round. One morning Lucy found a piece of thick course rope which she playfully tied on her arm. After a while this hurt, "Look," she pointed at the red mark, "let's wear a piece, that'll make a good sacrifice. What d'you think?"

No sooner said than done, the rope was divided into three and tied round their waists next to the skin. Because of being too tight, tears often streamed down Jacinta's face, yet she refused to loosen it.

"I want to offer it for sinners," is all she said.

Another sacrifice they mutually agreed upon was to strike their legs with stinging nettles, and this they did frequently.

By September 13th, news of the apparitions had spread throughout Portugal. The hostile publicity having had a reverse effect, 30,000 pilgrims swarmed into Fatima.

The path leading from Aljustrel to the Cova da Iria was crowded as the two girls wearing blue dresses and white veils set out with Francisco. Were it not for a handful of stalwart bystanders who forged a passage, it is doubtful whether they would have reached their destination.

An area near the holm oak had been cleared and Lucy began praying. The atmosphere was intense and necks craned heavenwards looking for the celestial visitor.

With the familiar flash came cries of joy. Many sprung to their feet pointing towards a brilliant globe above them; as usual the sun dimmed and the air became cooler. An awesome silence fell.

"What do you want of me?" Spoke Lucy.

"Continue to say the rosary to bring about an end to the war. In October Our Lord will come also, and Our Lady of Sorrows and Our Lady of Mount Carmel; St. Joseph and the child Jesus will bless the world. God is pleased with your sacrifices but does not want you sleeping with the rope on; wear it only during the day."

"They have begged me to ask you so many things; the cure of some sick persons, a deaf mute...."

"Yes, some I will cure, others not."

"The people would like a chapel built here."

"Use half the money collected on the biers for Our Lady of the Rosary. The other half you can use to build a chapel."

"So many still say I'm a liar and want to kill me."

"In October I shall perform a miracle so that all may believe." It was over; slowly the Lady ascended.

When there was nothing more to see the favoured ones were hemmed in by those present who wanted to be told the Lady's words; they were rescued however by their fathers.

Though the Church authorities remained aloof, some members of the clergy took matters into their own hands and subjected the seers to repeated interrogations. Many utterly opposed the children and did their best to wring out a confession of denial. Failing to do so they took their anger out on the seers' parents; nevertheless a few were courteous and open-minded. Among these was a Father Manuel Nunes Formigão, Professor of Theology at Santarem Seminary. Having a great devotion to Our Lady of Lourdes, he was incredulous on first hearing of the alleged apparitions and feared that his promise of promoting devotion to her in Portugal was in jeopardy. He decided however to give it some thought and be present at the Cova on September 13th.

On this day, standing some distance away, he noticed nothing unusual, and classed as normal the dimming light and cooler air, going away disbelieving, though determined to find out more.

Two weeks later he returned to Aljustrel and questioned the seers one by one: Franciso was first.

"Well, lad, what did you see at the Cova da Iria?"

"I saw Our Lady," Francisco replied.

"Whereabouts?"

"On top of the holm oak tree."

"Does she appear suddenly or does she come from somewhere?"

"I saw her come from where the sun is and she stops over the holm oak."

"Does she come slow or fast?"

"She always comes fast."

"Do you hear what she says to Lucy?"

"No, nothing at all."

"Have you ever spoken to the Lady or does she speak to you?"

"No, I've never asked her anything and she only speaks to Lucy.

"Does she smile?"

"No, she's always serious."

"What does she wear?"

"A long dress with a cloak over her head; it's as long as her dress."

"What colour are her clothes?"

"They're white and there's some gold stripes".

"What posture does she take...how does she stand?"

"Like someone praying."

"Has she anything in her hands?"

"Yes, a rosary....it's all white, and she holds it between the palm and back of her hands."

"Has she anything in her ears?"

"I don't know, her ears are covered by the cloak."

"Is the Lady nice to look at?"

"Oh, she is; she's very pretty."

"Prettier than that girl?" The priest pointed to a girl dressed in white.

"Much...she's prettier than anyone I've ever seen."

Francisco was dismissed and Jacinta called in. Putting the stool beside him Father Formigão said kindly, "Sit down here....Now, Jacinta, tell me, is it right you saw Our Lady on the thirteenth day of each month since May?"

"Yes," she said quietly.

"Where did she come from?"

"From heaven where the sun is."

"What did she wear?"

"A white dress embroidered in gold, and a white cloak."

"What colour is her hair?"

"I don't know, it's covered up."

"And earrings....does she wear those?"

"I couldn't see her ears."

"How does she hold her hands?"

"Like this." The small girl joined her hands as if to pray.

"Is the rosary in her left or right hand?"

"Her right."

"Are you sure?" The priest then proceeded to try and catch the child out but in the end only confused her and she was unable to answer.

"What did the Lady tell Lucy you must do?"

"Say the rosary every day."

"Well, do you?"

"Oh, yes, every day, with Lucy and Francisco."

"Alright, little one, you can go now."

By this time Lucy had come back from the vineyards where she was helping out. Although exhausted from continual questioning, the girl remained quite calm and polite.

"Is it right that Our Lady appeared to you at the Cova da Iria?"

"Yes."

"How many times has she appeared?"

"Five."

"On what day?"

"On the thirteenth, except when we were kidnapped and taken to Ourem...then she came to Valhinos."

"Is it correct that you said Our Lady appeared to you last year?"

"No, Senhor Padre, She did not come last year or before May this year."

"Which direction does she come from? Is it the East?"

"I don't know. She stands above the holm oak and then she goes away towards where the sun rises."

"How long does she stay with you?"

"Not very long."

"Long enough to say an 'Our Father' and Hail Mary'?"

"Oh, longer than that, Senhor Padre. Although sometimes she stays longer than others."

"Were you frightened the first time you saw her?"

"I was frightened but not of her, only the thunderstorm I thought we were going to have."

"What sort of clothes did she have on?"

"A white dress and a cloak which went over her head. Both came down nearly to her feet."

"Had the dress any decoration?"

"Two golden cords hang from her neck to about her waist where they join together in a little gold ball."

"Is there anything round the waist?"

"No."

"Does she wear earrings?"

"Little gold ones, but the light is very bright just there where her cloak is, so I could be mistaken."

"She has a rosary...which hand is it in?"

"The right one."

"Was it five or fifteen decades?"

"I don't know."

"Was there a cross on it?"

"Yes, a white cross....the beads and chain were white as well."

"How about her name, have you asked her?"

"Yes, and she's going to tell us in October."

"Where does she come from...did you ask her that?"

"I did on June 13th. She said from heaven."

"Is she smiling when you see her or has she a sad face?"

"She's not either. She is always serious."

"Have you and your cousins been told to pray?"

"Yes, we have, we must say the rosary to obtain peace for the world."

"Did she say people must go to the Cova?"

"No, she didn't mention it."

"Now this secret....are you sure you're forbidden to tell anyone?"

"I am quite sure."

"Is it only to do with you or all three of you?"

"The three of us, Senhor Padre."

"Surely you can tell your confessor!" The girl remained silent and the priest left the matter alone.

"Is it right the Lady told you to learn to read?"

"Yes, she told me that when she appeared the second time."

"But I understood that she is going to take you to heaven soon; in that case it isn't worth it."

"I've never told anyone she's going to take me to heaven soon, so it's untrue."

"How about the money people leave at the holm oak?"

"It's to be used for bringing devotion to Our Lady of the Rosary; the rest for a chapel."

"Where is this chapel to be?"

"I don't know, she never said."

"Are you pleased Our Lady appeared to you?"

"Oh yes I am, Senhor Padre."

"Is Our Lady coming on the thirteenth again?"

"Yes, so is St. Joseph and the infant Jesus. They're going to bless the world and soon there'll be peace."

"What else did she say?"

"She said in October she'll perform a miracle so that

people will believe she appeared to us."

"Were you taught any prayers?"

"She told us to say at the end of each decade, *Oh my Jesus, forgive our sins, save us from the fires of hell, lead all souls to heaven especially those in most need.*

Here ended the first of many interviews with Fr. Formigão. Though the children seemed genuine enough, he still felt it was in their imagination.

CHAPTER ELEVEN

"IT'S ABSOLUTE MISERY"

The door was opened by Maria-Rosa.

"Bom dia, Senhora," Fr. Formigão raised his hat, "I'm going to question the children again, let's see if we can sort out this wretched business."

The woman looked relieved to see him. With only two days to go before the thirteenth she was more worried than ever. Rumour had it that their homes were to be burned down and bombs planted in the Cova; already the village was seething with hatred and tension.

"Come in, come in, Senhor Padre." She seated him and brought some refreshment. Drinking his wine the priest availed himself of the opportunity to question Maria-Rosa, who was more than willing to oblige.

"What connection is there between your daughter and the Marto children?"

"They are cousins, Senhor Padre, my husband and their mother are brother and sister."

"Who told you Our Lady appeared at the Cova, was it your daughter?"

"No, she said nothing...I had to drag it out of her when this wild story came back to me."

"Did you tell her not to go to the Cova after that?"

"Well, no, not really."

"How come they were out in the fields anyway, did they go with other children?"

"No, they went on their own, Senhor Padre...they had sheep to look after."

"I believe you are the only one in the village who can read?" The woman nodded. "And that you read stories to the village children?" Another nod from Maria-Rosa. "Then you no doubt told them about the apparitions at La Salette?"

"I have read that story but only to my own family."

"Didn't Lucy ever mention La Salette or the visionaries? Isn't it possible it made an impression on her?"

"She never mentioned it."

"When the Administrator imprisoned the three cousins, did you do anything about it?"

She shook her head, "Manuel Marto sent one of his boys to see if they were there, not to fetch them back though."

"Do you have many visitors?"

Maria-Rosa threw her arms in the air, "Oh, Senhor Padre, it's absolute misery. We get no peace at all. All the time people come demanding to speak to Lucy, to question her. We're a poor family, and this business is making us even poorer."

Father Formigão looked at her puzzled.

"Well, first there's the loss of the Cova. At one time we grew vegetables there, and it was good grazing ground. Then with so many priests coming I do nothing else but send one of my daughters to stay with the sheep while Lucy comes back and answers their questions...it wastes so much time, and that means money. Anyway we've got rid of the sheep now, except three, so that's an end to it."

"I see, I see," the priest nodded, "Oh well, the quicker we crack this thing the better."

Afterwards Lucy was brought and minutely examined, then the priest proceeded to the Marto household, doing the same to Francisco and Jacinta.

Though reserving his judgement he went away this time in a different frame of mind. He could not forget how at ease the youngsters were in his company, their eyes exuding the deep calm of interior peace and tranquillity. Above all he was taken aback by the phraseology they had used in imparting the Lady's messages. How could children of no education and tender years use words which were normally the domain of priests and theologians alike!

The Santos Home

CHAPTER TWELVE

THE MIRACLE

Maria-Rosa sat up in bed terror stricken quite certain that today October 13th was her last. A group of pilgrims passing by the house singing hymns had woken her from a fitful sleep. Throwing a shawl around her shoulders she rushed into Lucy's room.

"Lucy, Lucy, wake up quickly, we must go to confession. I'm worried sick, you and your miracle, they'll kill us for sure when it doesn't happen."

Already wide awake her daughter answered, "If you want to go to confession, Mama, I'll come with you by all means, but I have no doubts at all; I know the Lady will keep her promise. There *will* be a great miracle today."

Though her mother's spirits remained low, Lucy's confidence was slightly reassuring and she decided against confession and began her house duties.

The rain which had been falling in torrents all night long, showed no signs of abating and the heavy dark clouds which seemed to presage doom, all added to Senhora Santos' depression.

Despite unending interruptions by well wishers, Lucy, wearing the same outfit as the month previous, was ready. Her father and mother for the first time decided to accompany her quite openly. Anticipating delays they set off early, calling at the Marto's on the way.

Scenes were as last month; people knelt and prostrated before the seers beseeching favours; not even the swamp-like conditions deterred them. Progress was slow; eventually a man picked up Jacinta forcing his way through. Seeing her father struggling along behind, crushed on all sides, she began crying, afraid he might be hurt.

The seers arrived in good time, and Lucy, her mother

Jacinta after Miracle of Sun

kneeling behind her, Francisco, with Jacinta now a little calmer, placed between them, stood before the holm oak. Jacinta's father managed to get there too, but Antonio Santos was swallowed up in the crowds.

There was no delay. Lucy called out, "Put down your umbrellas, we must say the rosary." Quite unmindful of the pouring rain they obeyed. Shortly after came the familiar flash of light; the Lady was present.

"What do you want of me?"

"I want you to tell them to build a chapel here in my honour. I am the Lady of the Rosary. Let them continue to say the rosary every day. The war is going to end with the soldiers returning soon to their homes."

"I have many favours to ask you, the cure of sick persons, the conversion of some sinners, and other things."

"Some yes, others no. It is necessary that they amend their lives and ask pardon for their sins." Her face became grave and she continued, *"Let them offend Our Lord no more, for he is already much offended."* Then opening her hands she let the light emerging from them shine up towards the sun; slowly she too rose in its direction.

"Look at the sun," Lucy cried out. There the three seers saw a vision of St. Joseph holding the child Jesus, and Our Lady dressed in white with a blue cloak. St. Joseph and the infant blessed the world by making the sign of the cross. After this vision came another; Our Lord now as a man appeared, accompanied by his mother as Our Lady of Sorrows. This vision vanished to be replaced with one of Our Lady of Mount Carmel.

Though none but the children saw these revelations everyone stared at the sun which, like a great colossus had wrenched apart the rain laden clouds. Without warning its clearcut disc, radiant as lustrous pearl, began to rotate. Whirling at ever increasing speed, explosions of different colours spun off its circumference until it resembled a giant catherine wheel, its hues reflecting dramatically on the earth below. When the light turned a jaundiced yellow, the sun with great ferocity shook itself off its axis, gyrating madly in a zig zag pattern, until decreasing in momentum it hovered tantalisingly, before plunging towards the earth, increasing dramatically in size until the great explosive fireball obliterated all else.

Overcome with terror people flung themselves down, begging God's mercy and forgiveness, quite convinced the world was ending. Others said the Creed or the Hail Mary. When it seemed that the planets would collide in one horrendous fiery cataclysm, the sun, as if drawn by some invisible magnet, was restored to its place in the firmament.

People gasped breathelessly at the prodigious spectacle of God's might. Men bared their heads in awe, others lay on the ground which only seconds before had been flooded; now like their clothes it was bone dry.

The marvel ended and everyone was alive; laughter mingled with tears as they endeavoured to get near the visionaries.

"What did Our Lady say? What did she say?" Lucy in the protective arms of a big built man gesticulated wildly trying to get out the message.

Back at the Marto's house, where all three were taken, it was no different. Questions came from all angles, and the seers were observed like some strange animals that the crowd had come to watch, clambering on furniture and standing on beds as they did so, much to the consternation of Olympia.

Fr. Formigão, who had witnessed the miracle, came once more to talk to them. Eventually Lucy was taken home, but uninvited visitors followed in her wake and queued up to question her, until the child, completely exhausted, sunk to the floor, and fell fast asleep.

CHAPTER THIRTEEN

AMAZING EVENTS

The automobile moved slowly as it made its way to the station at Chão de Macas. The road was crowded but Avelino d'Almeida did not particularly mind, and he passed the time looking out on the lighthearted groups of peasants returning to harvest the grapes. Their light gait, smiling faces and bright eyes gave ample testimony to their love of God. Perhaps he envied them.

His reason for coming here was to bury dead once and for all these superstitious goings on. Director of the influential daily newspaper 'O Seculo', he had written a scathing article which ironically appeared in this morning's edition. In it he condemned the apparitions as being fraudulent. Now he was not so sure!

Standing on the perimeter road he saw it all. Even without the sun dancing, the multitude's faith alone cast long dark shadows of doubt across his atheistic heart.

But the sun had danced and the promised miracle occurred. Let science prove otherwise! Could he write that though? What effect would it have on his readers? Could a newspaper of national repute and strong republican sympathies write anything favourable about religion and Fatima in particular?

On the train to Lisbon Senhor d'Almeida was no nearer to solving it. In his house that night he roamed around sleepless, then, unable to delay it any longer, he sat at his writing desk. He was a journalist first, had always been a journalist, and whatever the recriminations would never betray his professional integrity. Under the glare of a lamp the following account which appeared in 'O Seculo' on October 15th 1917, was written.

O MILAGRE DE FÁTIMA

Varios aspectos do povo ajoelhado e orando no momento de descôbrir o sol e de se dar o fenomeno que tanto impressionou a multidão.

(Carta a alguem que pede um testemunho insuspeito).

Quebrando um silencio de mais de vinte anos e com a invocação dos longinquos e saudosos tempos em que convivemos n'uma fraternal camaradagem, iluminada então pela fé comum e fortalecida por identicos propositos, escreves-me para que te diga, sincera e minuciosamente, o que vi e ouvi na charneca de Fátima, quando a fama de celestes aparições congregou n'aquele desolado ermo dezenas de milhares de pessoas mais sedentas, segundo creio, de sobrenatural do que impelidas por mera curiosidade ou receosas de um logro... Estão os catolicos em desacordo sobre a importancia e a significação do que presencearam. Uns convenceram-se de que se tinham cumprido prometimentos do Alto; outros acham-se ainda longe de acreditar na incontroversa realidade de um milagre. Foste um crente na tua juventude e deixaste de sel-o. Pessoas de familia arrastaram-te a Fátima, no vagalhão colossal d'aquele povo que ali se juntou a 13 de outubro. O teu racionalismo sofreu um formidavel embate e queres estabelecer uma opinião segura socorrendo-te de depoimentos insuspeitos como o meu, pois que estive lá apenas no desempenho de uma missão bem dificil, tal a de relatar imparcialmente para um grande diario, *O Seculo*, os factos que diante de mim se desenrolassem e tudo quanto de curioso e de elucidativo a eles se prendesse. Não ficará por satisfazer o teu desejo, mas decerto que os nossos olhos e os nossos ouvidos não viram nem ouviram coisas diversas, e que raros foram os que ficaram insensiveis á grandeza de semelhante espectaculo, unico entre nós e de todo o ponto digno de meditação e de estudo...

*
* *

O que ouvi e me levou a Fátima? Que a Virgem Maria, depois da festa da Ascenção, aparecera a tres crianças que apascentavam gado, duas mocinhas e um zagalete, recomendando-lhes que orassem e prometendo-lhes aparecer ali, sobre uma azinheira, no dia 13 de cada mez, até que em outubro lhes daria qualquer sinal do poder de Deus e faria revelações. Espalhou-se a nova por muitas leguas em redondez : voou, de terra em terra, até os confins de Portugal, e a roma-

O'Seculo Newspaper

AMAZING EVENTS. HOW THE SUN DANCED AT MIDDAY IN FATIMA

Along the road from the Chão de Macas station we met the first groups going to the holy place, a distance of more than ten miles.

Men and women walked along, most of them barefoot, with the women carrying bags on their heads, topped with their heavy shoes, while the men leaned on their sturdy staffs and carried umbrellas as a precaution. They seemed unaware of all that happened around them, disinterested in either the landscape or the other wayfarers, saying the rosary in sad rhythm, as if immersed in a dream. A woman broke out with the first part of the 'Hail Mary', the greeting, and her companions took up in chorus the second part, the supplication. With slow, cadenced steps, they threaded their way along the dusty road, among pine groves and olive orchards, so that they might arrive before nightfall at the place of the apparitions. There, in the open, under the cold light of the stars, they planned to sleep and get the best places next day near the blessed holm oak, and thus have a better view.

As they entered the town of Vila Nova de Ourem, some women, already infected by the germ of atheism, joked about the great event.

"Aren't you going tomorrow to see the saint?" One asked.

"Me? No! Not unless she comes to see me!"

They laughed heartily, while the devout passed on, indifferent to anything that was not the motive of their pilgrimage. Only by a sheer stroke of luck or kindness could lodging be found in Ourem. All night long the most varied types of vehicles moved into the town square, carrying the faithful and the curious, as well as the old ladies somberly dressed, weighed down by the years but with the ardent fire of faith shining in their eyes, which gave them heart to leave for a day the little corner in the home from which they were inseparable.

At dawn new groups surged, undaunted, and crossed through the village without stopping for a moment, breaking the early morning silence with their beautiful hymns, the delicate harmony of the women's voices making a violent contrast with their rustic appearance.

The sun was rising, though the skies presaged a storm. Dark clouds loomed directly over Fatima. Nothing would stop the crowds converging from every direction on towards the holy place, utilizing every means of transport. Luxurious automobiles glided swiftly along the road, their horns sounding continually, while ox-carts dragged slowly alongside them. There were carriages of all types, victoria chaises, landaus, and wagons fitted out with seats for the occasion and crowded to the limit. Besides food, simple fare according to their modest needs, almost all brought a bundle of straw for the animals, which the 'poor man' of Assisi called our brothers, and which carried out their task so bravely. Once in a while one could see a small wagon trimmed with ornaments, small bells jingling softly as it moved along, yet the festive mood was discreet; there was composure of manner and perfect order. Donkeys trotted along the side of the road, and countless cyclists performed real feats to keep from colliding with vehicles.

By ten o'clock the sky was completely hidden behind the clouds, and the rain began to fall in earnest. Swept by the strong wind and beating upon the faces of the people, it soaked the roadway and the pilgrims to the marrow of their bones, unprotected as they were against the weather. But no one complained or turned back, and if some took shelter under trees and wells, the great majority continued on their journey with remarkable indifference to the rain. Some of the women had their garments so thoroughly soaked and clinging to their bodies that their figures showed through, as if they had just stepped out of the bath.

The place where the Virgin has alleged to have appeared is fronted to a large extent by the road which leads to Leiria, along which the vehicles bringing the pilgrims were parked. More than a hundred cars could be counted, more than a hundred bicycles, and countless numbers of other type of conveyance, among which was a bus from Torres Novas bringing a group of people of every social condition. But the great mass of people coming from great distances, the Minho and Beira in the north, Alentejo and Algarve in the south, conregated round the holm oak tree, which, according to the children, was the pedestal chosen by the Virgin. It could be considered the centre of a large circle round which spectators gathered to watch events.

Seen from the road, the general effect was picturesque. The peasants, sheltering under their huge umbrellas, accompanied the unloading of their provisions with the singing of hymns and the recitation of decades of the rosary in a matter-of-fact way. People plodded through the sticky clay in order to see the famous holm oak tree, with its wooden arch and hanging lanterns, at closer quarters. The groups alternated in singing the praises of the Virgin, and at one moment a terrified hare ran through the crowd, hardly noticed except by half a dozen small boys, who caught it and killed it.

Where were the little shepherds? Lucy, 10 years old, and her little companions, Francisco 9, and Jacinta 7, had not yet arrived. Finally, about half an hour before the time when the apparition

gem dos crentes foi aumentando de mez para mez, a ponto de se juntarem na charneca de Fátima, em 13 de outubro, umas cincoenta mil pessoas, consoante os calculos de individuos desapaixonados. Nas precedentes reuniões de fieis, não faltou quem tivesse suposto ver singularidades astronomicas e atmos-

1.—O povo abrigando-se sob os seus guarda-chuvas, em torno do local do milagre

fericas que se tomaram como indicio da imediata intervenção divina. Houve quem falasse de subitos abaixamentos de temperatura, da scintilação de estrelas em pleno meio dia e de nuvens lindas e jámais vistas em torno do sol. Houve quem repetisse e propalasse comovidamente que a Senhora recomendava penitencia, que pretendia a ereção de uma capela n'aquele local, que em 13 de outubro manifestaria, por intermedio de uma prova sensivel a todos, a infinita bondade e a omnipotencia de Deus...

Foi assim que, no dia celebre e tão anciado, afluiram de perto e de longe a Fátima, arrostando com todos os embaraços e todas as durezas das viagens, milhares e milhares de pessoas, umas que palmilharam leguas ao sol e á chuva, outras que se transportaram em variadissimos veiculos, desde os quasi pre-

historicos até os mais recentes e maravilhosos modêlos de automoveis, e ainda muitas mais que suportaram os incomodos das terceiras classes dos comboios, dentro das quaes, para percorrer hoje relativamente pequenas distancias, se perdem longas horas e até dias e noites? Vi ranchos de homens

e de mulheres, pacientemente, como enlevados n'um sonho, dirigirem-se, de vespera, para o sitio famoso, cantando hinos sacros e caminhando descalços ao ritmo d'eles e á recitação cadenciada do terço do Rosario, sem que os importunasse, os demovesse, os desesperasse, a mudança quasi repentina do tempo, quando as bategas de agua transformaram as estradas poeirentas em fundos lamaçaes e ás doçuras do outono sucederam, por um dia, os asperrimos rigores do inverno... Vi a multidão, ora comprimida á volta da pequenina arvore do milagre e desbastando-a dos seus ramos para os guardar como reliquias, ora espraiada pela vasta charneca que a estrada de Leiria atravessa e domina e que a mais pitoresca e heterogenea concorrencia de carros e pessoas atravancou n'aquele dia memoravel, aguardar na melhor ordem as

O'Seculo Newspaper

would take place, their presence was noted. The girls wore wreaths of flowers and looked like angels as they moved towards the arch. The rain fell unceasingly, but nobody minded.

Latecomers were still arriving in cars. Groups of people were kneeling in the mud, quite unconcerned. Moved by an interior guidance, Lucy asked the people to shut their umbrellas, and in spite of the rain, she was promptly obeyed. There were so many people there, praying in such earnestness, almost in ecstasy as if their dry lips could no longer move, their hands joined, their eyes wide with wonder, people who seemed to be overpowered by the supernatural.

The child asserted that the Lady had spoken to her once more, and then the sky, still overcast, began to clear overhead. The rain ceased, and the sunlight illuminated the whole landscape with all the sombre effects of a wintry morning.

It was the hour by the sun that this multitude followed, a multitude calculated to reach at least forty thousand persons, as reckoned by various disinterested people of culture who were unaffected by any mystical influence. The miraculous manifestation, the visible sign previously announced, was about to take place, many pilgrims asserted....and then they witnessed a spectacle so unique as to be unbelievable for anyone other than an eye witness.

From the road, where the vehicles were parked and where hundreds of people who had not dared to brave the mud were congregated, one could see the immense throng turn towards the sun, which appeared free from clouds and at its zenith. It looked like a plaque of silver, and it was possible to look at it without the least discomfort. It neither burned nor blinded the eyes. Some said it was an eclipse taking place. But at that moment a great shout went up and one could hear the spectators nearest at hand shouting: 'A miracle! A miracle! Marvel! Marvel!'

Before the astonished eyes of the crowd, whose aspect was biblical as they stood bareheaded, pale with fright, eagerly searching the sky, the sun trembled, made sudden incredible movements outside all cosmic laws--the sun 'danced' according to the typical expression of the people.

Standing at the step of the Torres Novas bus was an old man, whose appearance in face and figure reminded one of Paul Deroulede. With his face turned to the sun he recited the creed in a loud voice. I saw him afterwards going up to those around him who still had their hats on, and vehemently imploring them to uncover their heads before such an extraordinary demonstration of the existence of God. Identical scenes were repeated elsewhere, and in one place a woman cried out in a gasp of surprise: 'How dreadful there are some men who do not even bare their heads before such a stupendous miracle!' People then began to ask each other what they had seen. The great majority admitted to having seen the trembling and the dancing of the sun. Others affirmed that they had seen the face of the blessed Virgin, while others, again, swore that the sun whirled on itself like a giant catherine wheel and that it lowered itself to the earth as if to burn it in its rays. Some said they saw it change colours successively.

It was almost three o'clock in the afternoon. The sky was swept of clouds and the sun followed its course in its usual splendour, so that no one ventured to gaze at it directly. What about the little shepherds?

Lucy, who had spoken to Our Lady, was announcing with expressive gestures as she was carried along shoulder high by a man and passed from group to group, that the war would end and that the soldiers would return. But news like that, however, did nothing to increase the jubilation of those who heard it. The heavenly sign was for them sufficient: it was everything.

Intense curiosity prevailed to see the two little girls in their wreaths of roses, and to kiss the hands of these little saints, one of whom, Jacinta, seemed nearer to fainting than dancing. They had so longed to see the sign from heaven, they had seen and were satisfied, and radiated their burning faith. Travelling salesmen were offering postcards with the children's photographs, and even a statue of the Virgin as being the figure in the vision.

The crowds dispersed rapidly, without any difficulty, without any sign of disorder, without any need for policemen to regulate them. Those who were the first to arrive were also the first to depart, running out on the roadway, travelling on foot with their footwear in a bundle on their heads or strung from their staffs. They went with hearts overflowing with joy, to bring the good news to their hamlets, which for the time being had been depopulated.

What of the priests? Some turned up at the place, mingling more among the curious spectators rather than among the pilgrims avid for heavenly signs and favours. Perhaps neither one nor the other succeeded in concealing their happiness, which so often transpired in triumphant guise. It remained for the competent to do justice to the bewildering dance of the sun which, on this day in Fatima, caused 'Hosannas' to resound from the hearts of the faithful present and naturally made a great impression, as people worthy of belief assured me, on the free thinkers and others without any religious conviction who had come to this now famous spot on the poor pasture lands high up in the Serra d'Aire.

Keeping Our Lord company

CHAPTER FOURTEEN

"I SHALL SPEND MY HEAVEN...."

"Is Lucy back from school yet?" Father Ferreira asked, sinking into a chair.

"Not yet, Senhor Padre, though she should be here any moment."

Refusing the offered glass of wine, the priest brushed the dust from his cassock and straightened the long garment over his crossed knees.

"This business is getting me down." His face registered displeasure, "as if I haven't got enough work to do in this scattered parish without these so called apparitions on my door-step; if that isn't enough, I have to obey the Cardinal Patriarch and investigate them....but let me tell you, Senhora, I find it very distasteful."

Maria-Rosa nodded in sympathy. "D'you think the Church will ever approve them?"

"Goodness knows, depends on the findings."

"Once I told myself," the woman mused, "that if one other person saw Our Lady, I'd believe....now lots of people say they saw her in that globe of light! Then there's this business about the sun, which I saw with my own eyes, yet still I'm torn apart; one day I believe, the next day I don't...and that's how it'll always be, unless of course the Church says Our Lady appeared here."

Now extremely disgruntled the priest spoke as if to himself. "Our Blessed Mother wouldn't choose children as young as these; surely she'd have shown herself to grown up sensible people. What really annoys me is all these simpletons who prostrate themselves in prayer on a piece of waste land, while their living God....the God of all altars in the Blessed Sacrament is left alone and abandoned in the tabernacle. Why do they leave money without any purpose under the holm oak? I've had to stop the repairs on my church because I've no money to pay for them; my blood boils at the thought. No, if there was any truth in the matter the church would fare better."

Maria-Rosa's temper came to the surface. "All these grumbles about your church, Senhor Padre. What about me and my household? What good has it done us? None. Our work has come to a standstill. We're interrupted every day by callers, my house isn't my own any more, they come and stare at us, peer through the windows, trample all over the place...and of course the endless questions." Warming to her subject she went on, "Look how often you send for my Lucy because some priest or other wants to see her; she's spent more time in your presbytery than with our sheep. I told Padre Formigão the same...we had in the end to follow the Martos' example and sell the flock...And," she wagged a finger, "don't forget that the land they prostrate themselves on is *our* land and the crops they've destroyed are *our* crops."

At this point the three seers came in, and a look of dismay momentarily crossed Lucy's face on seeing Father Ferreira. She knew what this meant, more questions. How sick she was of it all, day in and day out interminable inquisitions. Nevertheless she greeted him politely.

"Bom dia, Senhor Padre."

"The others can go, I only want to see you," he replied, "come and sit by me."

Thankful at being reprieved, Francisco and Jacinta needed no second telling and scuttled off.

Resigning herself to the inevitable Lucy sat down on a stool and answered him mechanically. When he eventually released her, she hastened to join her cousins who were sitting on the doorstep of their house anxiously awaiting her.

"Oh Lucy," Jacinta kissed her cousin, "you've been such a long time."

"Yes, I know; Oh how I wish we'd be left in peace. I've told Padre Ferreira everything over and over again and still he asks the same questions, and doesn't believe me."

Priests who at one time visited the Cova incognito, now did so quite openly. Consequently the seers were subjected to more rigorous examination.

One day, after a particularly hard time from one such priest whose questions were full of snares, Lucy was in a quandary, so much so that she consulted her cousins.

"I don't know whether we're doing right or wrong in not telling everything when people ask 'Did Our Lady tell you anything else?' I'm not sure if it's lying to keep things to ourselves as well as the proper secret. What do you think?"

"I don't know," Jacinta answered, "you're the one who wants these things kept to ourselves."

"Well, of course," Lucy retorted, "otherwise they'll all want to know what mortifications we practise! That would be the last straw! Now look, if you hadn't opened your mouth, no one would even know we'd seen Our Lady and spoken to her, just as they don't know about the angel.

"That's right," said Francisco, "you should have kept quiet."

"I'm sorry, Lucy, please forgive me."

She did, but this still left the problem unresolved, until one day a priest came who inspired her confidence; Lucy put her worry to him.

"Well, my child," he said, "when you are asked did Our Lady tell you anything else, say, yes she did, she also told us not to tell it to anyone, therefore we cannot tell you."

So fatigued were the seers that they began dodging visitors, and whenever possible hid away. One day while sitting on the Marto doorstep they noticed some strangers coming in their direction, "Quick, under the beds," Lucy jumped to her feet, followed by Francisco. Jacinta stayed where she was. "C'mon," Lucy said, running into the house.

"I'm not coming, I won't hide myself, I'll offer this sacrifice to Our Lord." Sometime later the visitors left.

"What did you say when they asked you where we were?" The eldest seer leaned over the small girl still seated on the steps.

"I didn't say anything, I just bowed my head, fixed my eyes on the ground and said nothing. I always do this when I don't want to tell the truth. I don't want to tell a lie either, because that's a sin."

"Let's go to the well," Francisco suggested, "there's more peace." He ran on ahead, but was soon back. "Hurry, hurry, there's some ladies coming." Without further ado all three clambered into the branches of a nearby fig tree; Jacinta did not hesitate this time, one sacrifice was enough without having to endure another fast on its heels! Their ploy worked and the ladies passed by, unable because of their large-brimmed hats to see anything above head height: once out of sight the rascals hurried from the tree and hid in the cornfields.

This habit of hiding was another reason for Father Ferreira's animosity, but what caused him to complain most was their running away to escape from priests. When taken to task over this, Lucy explained that they did so because it was the priests who asked the same endless questions over and over again.

Time went by and each day saw the visionaries going about their business. They prayed the rosary, made sacrifices, and in the little cave at Cabeço they knelt with foreheads touching the ground repeating the angel's prayer.

When a school for girls opened in Fatima next to the church, Lucy was able to carry out the Lady's command. Though Jacinta was not told to learn to read she sometimes accompanied her cousin. Francisco went to the Boleiros school for boys.

One morning while on their way Lucy spoke of her married sister's visit the previous evening.

"Teresa came to see me. She was sent by a poor woman who wants us to pray for her son. He's been arrested and charged with a crime he didn't commit. She said that if he can't prove he's innocent, he'll be exiled or put in prison for years."

When they reached Fatima, Francisco, who had been listening in silence, broke in, "Look, the best thing is for you to go and get on with your learning. I'll stay with the hidden Jesus and talk to him about it."

"What about school?" His sister asked.

"Oh, don't worry about that, it's not worth the trouble learning to read if I'm going to heaven soon...I'd rather keep Our Lord company." So saying he walked happily into church and there he stayed tucked away behind the baptismal font gazing at the tabernacle until the girls called for him. After joining him in prayer the threesome made their way home across the fields to avoid sightseers. At the Santos household, however, two rather refined ladies who had refused to budge until seeing the visionaries, were waiting. After a brief chat they were satisfied and rose to leave. As Francisco had kept his accustomed silence, feeling that because he had heard nothing during the apparitions the other two were better qualified to answer questions, one of the ladies turned to him.

"What do you want to be when you grow up?....Do you want to be a carpenter?"

"No, ma'am."

"How about a soldier?"

"No."

"A doctor? Wouldn't you like to be a good doctor and make people better?"

"No, I wouldn't."

"Ah, it's a priest then, isn't it? That's what you want to be."

"No, ma'am, I don't want to be a priest. I don't want to be anything. I just want to die and go to heaven."

Towards the end of that year, 1918, the influenza epidemic which swept Europe struck down the whole of the Marto household, with the exception of Manuel Marto. Recovery for Francisco and Jacinta was slow, particularly as their little bodies were already weakened by regular acts of mortification.

After a few weeks in bed the seers were allowed up, and although still unwell they continued making sacrifices. Lucy, who had escaped the virus and spent whatever free time she could with her cousins, one day received an urgent message to go to them at once.

"Our Lady's been to see us," Jacinta burst out, "she's coming to fetch Francisco soon and take him to heaven."

This news made the boy happy, which deceived his parents into believing he was on the mend and they allowed him out for short walks. Except on one occasion, when he dragged himself painfully to the Cova, his footsteps always led him to church, where he sat with Jesus. After one such walk his father remarked, "Your eyes are bright son; I can see you're improving all the time. We'll make a strong man out of you yet."

"No, Papa," the boy replied wisely, "Out Lady is coming for me soon."

A relapse came fast on the tail of these words, bronchial pneumonia set in, and with a permanently high temperature, Francisco's condition deteriorated. The youngster's cheerful acceptance, however, fooled all but his two faithful companions. Time was running out, and during the last few weeks Lucy became her cousin's sole confidant and he eagerly looked forward to when she would arrive breathless, having run all the way from school. At his bedside they talked quietly and intimately.

"Did you give my regards to the hidden Jesus?"

"Yes, Francisco, I did."

"Oh Lucy, it hurts me so much that I can't go and stay with him any more, please always remember to go in my place." He paused, took hold of her hand and squeezed it, "D'you remember when my parents sold the sheep?" Lucy nodded. "Jacinta and I still used to get up early and go with you: you asked me why, remember?" Another nod and Francisco went on, "I said I don't know why. Before it didn't matter to me to be in your company, I only used to come because Jacinta asked me, but things changed, I couldn't sleep because I was in such a hurry to be with you..." Both children were thoughtful for a moment. Francisco broke the silence, "I still feel the same way, Lucy, only more so. I just love it when you're with me."

Lucy put her arm gently around his shoulder. "Are you suffering a great deal?"

"Yes, I am, but I suffer everything for Our Lord and Our Lady."

He shifted a little and reached beneath his pillow for the piece of rope he wore as a penance. It was not to be put on in bed Our Lady had said, nevertheless he always kept it to hand just in case he should get up for a while. Now he gave his cousin the rope and then fell back weakly on his pillows. "I do want to suffer more, Lucy, but I feel very sick; still it won't be long before I'm in heaven."

"Then make sure you pray very hard for sinners....and the Holy Father....and Jacinta and me...."

"Yes, I'll pray," he whispered, "but you'd better ask Jacinta for that. I'm sure I'll forget all about it. I'll be too busy comforting Jesus and Mary."

On April 3rd 1919, not quite eleven years old, Francisco Marto made his first communion; Our Lord visited him. The next day, in the early hours of the morning, they became inseparable for ever.

Jacinta's bedroom

CHAPTER FIFTEEN

LUCY'S MISSION

"Jacinta, dear," Olympia Marto said gently," we really must go now."

Locked in the arms of her cousin, the girl was crying bitterly, "Oh, Lucy, I'll never see you again, please pray for me."

Manuel Marto parted the weeping children; putting his frail emaciated daughter astride his shoulders, he left the house followed by Olympia, who carried Jacinta's small bag of personal belongings. Aljustrel was left behind as, waved on their way by a handful of neighbours, they took the path to Fatima. Arrangements had been made for a car to take them to the station at Chão de Macas, where mother and daughter would board the train for Lisbon. Once in hospital Jacinta was to have an operation, then the best medical attention to aid her recovery.

When Lucy could no longer see her aunt, uncle and cousin, she went directly to the well at the foot of her garden. Sheltered by fig and plum trees and cut off from the house by a rough stone wall, it had on many occasions formed an oasis of peace in troubled times, but never before had it witnessed Lucy so wretched.

Emotionally exhausted she sank to the ground and ran her fingers over the flagstones on which they had so often played; it seemed impossible to believe that those days were over. She still pined for Francisco, and now with Jacinta gone for good, her heart felt as though it would break.

"Lucy," the little girl had said one day, "Our Lady's been to see me. She told me I'm going to two hospitals; not to be cured though. I'm going to suffer a lot then die all on my own. She said I'm not to be afraid because she'll come and take me up to heaven....Oh, Lucy, pray a lot for me, I'm going to die alone....alone...."

Now Lucy's tears mixed with the water of the well as memories came flooding back, and so she would have remained had not her mother arrived on the scene.

"What, still crying, young lady? Come on, up you get, this cold January air won't do you any good." Lucy stood up slowly and Maria-Rosa held out a handkerchief;

"Here, dry your eyes, it's not the end of the world. Jacinta will have the best doctors in Lisbon, she'll soon be better, and back with us again."

Lucy looked into her mother's eyes and smiled sadly; she knew better.

They walked together as far as the farmhouse, but feeling irrisistably drawn, Lucy excused herself and made for the Martos' home once more.

Inside all was quiet, and going to Jacinta's room she seated herself on a stool beside the bed. Her hands reached out to touch the pillow, seeking her little suffering companion; they found nothing, slid gently over the bedspread and then stilled.

As if in sympathy, the rain which had threatened now fell in torrents, beating a tattoo on the window pane. Lucy heard nothing, her thoughts were miles away, recalling the past year.

Before Francisco died, when he and Jacinta were confined to their rooms, Lucy divided her time between them, though Jacinta invariably cut the visits short saying, "Go now, and sit with Francisco, I want to make the sacrifice of being alone."

"What other sacrifices have you made today, Jacinta?" Lucy would ask. Her answer was always the same, "A lot."

One day she remarked, "When Mama went out today, I so wanted to go and see Francisco, but I never went. I offered it up for sinners instead."

The death of Francisco caused the child great distress, and at times she remained silent for long stretches. When

Lucy questioned her one day she replied,

"I'm thinking of two things: Francisco and how much I'd like to see him again, and of that war which is coming, of so many people who are going to die and go to hell. What a shame! If they would stop offending God neither the war would come, nor would they go to hell. Look, Lucy, when you see that strange light in the sky, run to heaven."

"But," Lucy answered, "you know I can't do that; Our Lady said I've got to stay here."

"Oh, yes, so you have, well, don't be afraid, I'll pray for you, and the Holy Father, and for Portugal that the war won't come here....and I'll pray for all priests."

Even though she missed Francisco and was in agony with her illness, Jacinta continued to seek sacrifices. One day when her mother brought the customary cup of milk, the young invalid waved it away;

"I don't want to drink it, Mama."

"I don't know how to get her to take anything," said the frustrated woman, "she's no appetite at all."

"Why do you disobey your mother?" Lucy asked when the door closed after her. "Why don't you drink it and offer it up as a sacrifice to Our Lord?"

Tears glistened in the girl's eyes, "Oh, Lucy, I didn't think of that....Mama, Mama," she called, "bring back the milk, I've changed my mind." And when Olympia did so, her daughter swallowed it unflinchingly. Later she said, "If only you knew how hard it was to do that; it hurts me more and more to drink milk and soup, I get so many pains in my chest."

A tumour formed on her left lung, promptly followed by purulent pleurisy; she was eventually taken to hospital in Ourem, where she spent the months of July and August 1919. Prior to her departure she confided, "Our Lady asked me if I still wanted to convert more sinners and I said 'Yes'. She told me I'd go to hospital and after that I would be quite alone...dear Lucy, if only you could come with me, it's hard going away without you. Perhaps the hospital is a very dark house, where no one can see anything, and I must go down there to suffer alone. Still, it doesn't matter, I'll suffer for the love of Our Lord to make reparation to the Immaculate Heart of Mary, and for the conversion of sinners and for the Holy Father."

At Ourem hospital the treatment received was ineffectual, the tumour broke and she returned home with a large open wound in her side which discharged continuously. This needed washing out daily with a rubber syringe, which her untrained mother attended to. Jacinta suffered the daily dressing without a murmur.

Influenza, tuberculosis, pleurisy, and pneumonia—all gradually sapped the seer's strength. One morning Lucy found her even more pale and drawn than usual.

"Last night I had many aches and pains, and I decided to offer Our Lord the sacrifice of not turning in bed, well, I never slept a wink, I feel so weak. When I was by myself I used to get out of bed and say the angel's prayers, now, if I put my head on the floor I fall over."

By winter Jacinta was nothing but bones: It was suggested that one last effort be made to cure her; thus she went to the nation's capital. Jacinta knew of her fate long before the matter was raised.

"Lucy, do you remember Our Lady told me I shall go to another hospital in Lisbon...I shan't see you or my family again. Now you've got to stay here and reveal to the world that Our Lord wants to establish devotion to the Immaculate Heart of Mary. Everyone must take their petitions to her because Our Lord desires that His Heart be venerated with the Heart of His Mother. Tell them they should all ask for peace from the Immaculate Heart of Mary, as God has placed it in her hands...Oh, if only I could put in everyone's heart the fire that is in mine; it doesn't burn me, but makes me love so much the hearts of Jesus and Mary."

Lucy came back to the present with these words reverberating in her head.

No more time for moping, she had a job to do. Standing up, she looked once more around the room, shrugged into her cloak and, with a newly found determination, hastened off to get on with her learning!

"Surely you could see how sad Our Lady was last month"

PART TWO

"MAKE REPARATION FOR THEIR SINS AND CONSOLE YOUR GOD."

"Yes, Francisco will go to heaven, but first he must say many rosaries."

Though he saw the beautiful Lady, Francisco never heard her speak, and it soon dawned on him that, unlike Lucy and Jacinta, he must work hard to gain a place in heaven. On learning during the second apparition that he and Jacinta would not be left on earth long, he focused his whole attention on the task with a determination hitherto unknown.

Lucy admits in her memoirs that there was nothing about Francisco which attracted her, and had it not been for ties of kinship, they would have gone their separate ways. What irked the eldest seer most was her cousin's passive and indifferent nature; were it not for Jacinta dragging him around his time would have been idled away. In complete contrast to his little sister Francisco loved peace and would do anything for a quiet life!

"It seems to me," said Lucy, "if he grew up to be a man, his chief defect would be, 'Don't bother about it'."

On rare occasions when playing with the other lads he did not care whether he won or lost, in fact so obvious was his disinterest that he was eventually excluded from team games.

On being asked one day the whereabouts of a favourite hand-painted handkerchief, Francisco simply shrugged the matter off, "One of the boys stole it, it's of no interest to me."

When the cousins first went out with their sheep Lucy tried hard to break his lethargy. Hoping for at least a flicker of spunk she tyranically exerted her will, "Francisco, go and sit on that rock and don't move until I tell you." When later, feeling sorry she returned, it was only to find him sitting quite happily in the same spot. Nothing was achieved, for on being told to stand up, Francisco did so in good humour and joined in their game as if nothing had happened.

Where Lucy failed, Our Lady succeeded. But the road to heaven was to be a long upward climb for Francisco. Never given much to prayer except that imposed as a family duty, we find him eagerly joining the others and often encouraging them by his example; mindful always of the need for extra rosaries he never wasted a moment.

Towards the end of the series of apparitions Francisco had formed an intimate relationship with God, and when on October 13th he saw both Mary and Jesus looking so sad, he was distraught. Never were her parting words forgotten, "STOP OFFENDING GOD FOR HE IS ALREADY MUCH OFFENDED."

This is what she and the Angel before her had come to say. Francisco grasped their import immediately.

The thought of Our Lord, grief stricken at the sins of mankind, took Francisco over and his sole concern was to make up for them. Before the tabernacle in church this small boy sat quietly for hours on end, keeping company the Lord who was so unhappy and neglected. As far as he was concerned, his sister could get on with her job of converting sinners, and while she did so he would comfort God.

In the pastures it was his chief concern when an opportunity to be alone presented itself. Many a time the girls surprised him behind a wall or patch of brambles.

"Why don't you come and pray with us?" They asked.

"I'd rather pray by myself," he answered, "and to think of Our Lord so sad because of our sins."

"Francisco, which do you prefer, to console Jesus or convert sinners so they won't go to hell?"

"I'd rather console Jesus. Surely you could see how

Francisco's coffin and procession, from the cemetary to the Basilica followed by Mr. & Mrs. Marto, 1952

unhappy Our Lady was last month, and you know she told you people must stop offending God for he is already much offended. Well, I want to comfort him; after that I can pray for sinners."

This love of God showed in Francisco's relationship with people. Although shy and retiring he co-operated with those who after the apparitions interviewed him; he spoke with others seeking his advice, doing everything possible to help. What he did find difficult, however, was speaking to or seeing sick people, and preferred whenever possible to pray for them instead.

An indication of the boy's holiness was the attempts of the devil to trip him up. Failing to succeed, one day he showed his hatred for the young shepherd. The three of them were at a place called Pedreira. As the sheep grazed Lucy and Jacinta jumped from one cliff to another making their voices echo in the ravines. Francisco as usual went behind a rock to pray. Some time later the girls heard him calling for them and Our Lady. Worried as to what might have happened they ran to look for their companion and found him kneeling, unable to move because of fear. "What's wrong? What happened?" They chorused anxiously. Trembling and almost suffocated with fright he whispered, "It was one of those big animals from hell; it was sparking with fire."

This encounter with the devil made him even more determined to get to heaven. Seriously ill in bed he vouched that he would spend eternity consoling a God who like himself had feelings and was often hurt.

Francisco died with the rosary entwined around his fingers. He had said sufficient when he allowed God into his life.

"MANY GO TO HELL FOR THEY HAVE NOBODY TO SACRIFICE THEMSELVES AND PLEAD FOR THEM"

"There are people, even devout ones," stresses Lucy, "who are afraid to speak about hell to children lest they frighten them, but God did not hesitate to show it to three children, one of whom was only seven years old."

One cannot mitigate the effect of this vision on these children. So terrible and horrible was it that Lucy admits they would surely have died of fright had not Our Lady promised them heaven.

Jacinta was most affected by the anguish of lost souls that she determined to do all in her power to prevent people suffering this fate. She was quite unstinting in obeying Mary's demands for *penance and sacrifice* to save them.

"Oh hell, hell," she would moan, "how sorry I am for souls that go to hell! And people burn there alive like wood in a fire?"

While out with the sheep Jacinta spent a lot of time tossing this subject around her mind; invariably she turned to Lucy for explanations.

"Do people go to hell forever and not get out again?"

"Yes."

"Not even after many years?"

"No, hell never ends."

"And heaven too?"

"Whoever goes to heaven never leaves it."

"And whoever goes to hell doesn't either?"

"Yes, don't you see they are eternal and never end."

She was totally convinced that if everyone saw a vision of hell they would amend their lives. When thousands began

Jacinta after vision of Hell

coming to the Cova during the apparitions, the youngest seer felt it too good an opportunity to let pass.

"Oh, Lucy, you must tell that lady to show hell to these people when she comes to the Cova next month...you will see, they will be converted."

After the apparition, a little despondent, she asked;

"Why didn't Our Lady show hell to them?"

"I forgot to ask her," Lucy answered.

"I didn't remember either," she said sadly.

The vision of hell coupled with special graces received through Mary's Immaculate Heart gave the young girl a unique understanding of sin. As loathing for it increased, the more compassionate she became to the sinner; never condemning but doing all in her power to bring about a conversion. One incident is typical of the child.

In Aljustrel there was a woman who each time she saw the seers insulted them. One day they met her when she was leaving the tavern rather the worse for drink. Not content with hurling abuse, she beat them. When they managed to escape Jacinta was very serious, "We must ask Our Lady to help this poor woman, and we must offer sacrifices to save her. She says so many wicked things that if she doesn't confess she'll to go hell".

Some days later the woman in question accidently came upon Jacinta in prayer and so impressed was she by her composure that no further proof was necessary to convince her that the apparitions were real. She stopped abusing the children and frequently asked their intercession with Our Lady to forgive her sins.

Jacinta's personal qualities were to edify many. On being asked by a priest what she felt in her young cousin's company, Lucy replied, "What I felt was what one normally feels when one is with a holy person who seems to be communicating with God in everything. Jacinta had a serious, modest and affable character which seemed to translate the presence of God in all her acts, common in people already advanced in age and great virtue."

This goodness, however, did not prevent her from handing out reprimands when necessary. Lucy writes,

"If in her presence children or even adults said something wrong or performed an action less than proper, she reproached them saying; *'Don't do that, you are offending God and he is already much offended.'* If the person or child answered back calling her a fake, a holy Joe or a little worm-eaten saint, or something like that, which happened often, she would look at them with severity and walk away without saying another word."

Jacinta did what she considered her duty, accepting firmly on the chin every affront that came her way. It was riding the knocks that came from people and every day events, for the love of God, which saved most souls. Our Lady intimated this much when she appeared to Jacinta and her brother while they were ill. Francisco learnt he was soon to go to heaven; Jacinta was asked if she would be prepared to stay on earth longer and convert more sinners. When she agreed Mary told the small one that it entailed much suffering.

Although always in pain, the separation from home and loved ones caused her the most distress. Jacinta's stay in hospital at Ourem was only the prelude to her final parting and death in Lisbon. But one consolation awaited her there; the Mother of God re-appeared. That gave the visionary a final chance to ask a question that had for so long bothered her.

"What is it, what is it?" She used to ask Lucy, "What do people do that is so bad to make them go to such a dreadful place?"

The older girl did not know the answer, "Maybe it's telling lies or missing Mass, I don't know..."

Our Lady, however, gave the answer.

"The sin which causes the loss of most souls is that of impurity. People should avoid luxuries and do much

penance to break the habit of sin."

When Jacinta passed on these words she added, "Our Lady was very sad when she told me. Oh, I'm so sorry for her."

The low neck dresses and short skirts which some of the visitors and nurses wore prompted the girl to remind them to avoid immodest dress. The doctors too were reprimanded for their worldly behaviour.

Up until her last breath Jacinta did all in her power to lead people to the happiness of loving and being loved by God. She died alone, as Our Lady predicted, on February 20th, 1920, after weeks of slow crucifixion caused by her illness, which like Our Lord she offered up to save her *poor sinners.*

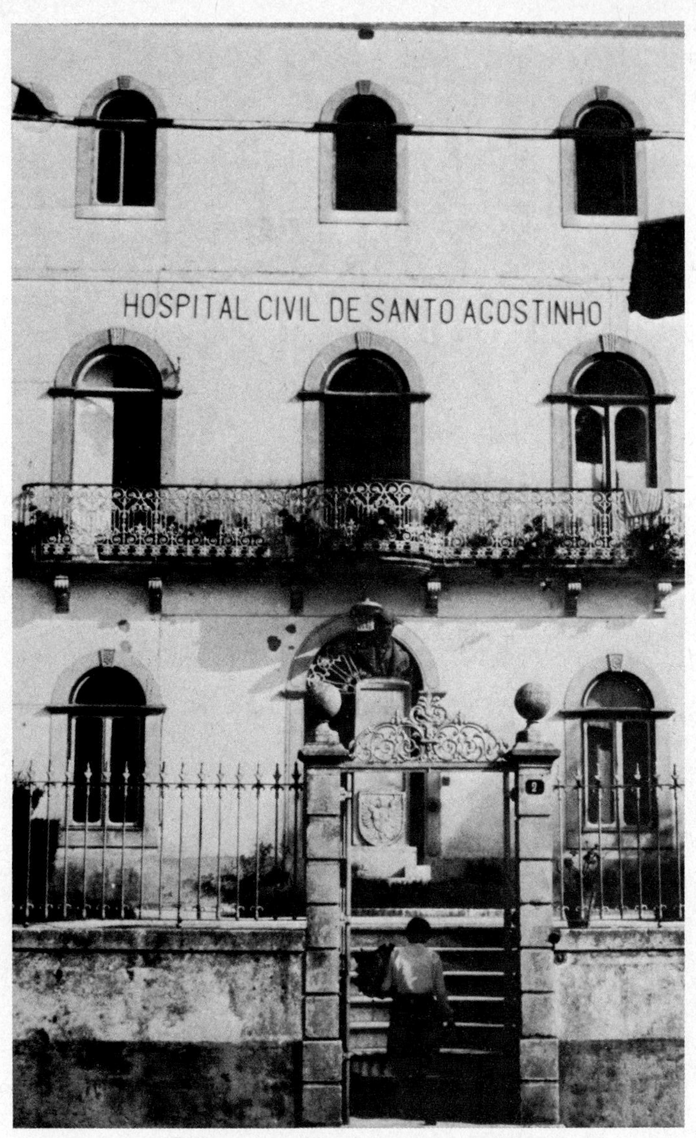

Hospital of St. Augustine, Vila Nova de Ourem

"IF MY REQUEST IS HEARD RUSSIA WILL BE CONVERTED".

In 1921, just over a year after Jacinta's death, Lucy left Aljustrel to continue her schooling with the Sisters of St. Dorothy at Oporto.

Four years later, with her education completed, Lucy expressed the desire to become a Dorothean nun; when accepted she began her postulancy at Pontevedra, Spain.

Within months of arriving, Lucy was privileged with another apparition. While in her cell on December 10th 1925, Our Lady, her Heart encircled with thorns, appeared; beside her, the child Jesus hovered above a luminous cloud. He spoke.

"Have pity on the Heart of your most holy Mother, which suffers at man's ingratitude; there is no one to console her."

Then His mother said, *"Look, my daughter, at my Heart pierced by thorns of blasphemy and ingratitude. You at least console me. Make known to the world that I promise to assist at the hour of death with all the graces necessary for salvation, those who on the first five consecutive months confess, receive Holy Communion and say the rosary, meditating for fifteen minutes on the mysteries with the intention of offering me reparation."*

In a subsequent apparition it was confirmed that one need not go to confession on the first five Saturdays, if in a state of grace, and further, the practice of the devotion will be equally acceptable on a Sunday following the first Saturday for a just reason.

After this apparition Lucy felt greatly perturbed, for the communions of reparation were included in the Fatima message designated *The Secret*. She was faced with months of anxiety regarding spreading this devotion until, towards the end of 1927, Our Lord gave permission for most of it to be made known.

The secret came in three parts, two of which were revealed to the seers during the July 13th apparition, prior to their imprisonment at Ourem. First the terrifying vision of hell, and second the consecration of Russia to Mary's Immaculate Heart.

When the Blessed Virgin announced the approaching end of World War One, she predicted the second, but said, "In order to prevent it, I will come and ask for Russia's consecration and the First Five Saturday communions."

With the propagation of the latter underway, Our Lady, in 1929, appeared to Lucy again.

"The moment has arrived. God wants the Holy Father and all the bishops of the world to consecrate Russia to my Immaculate Heart. He promises its conversion through this means."

On October 13th 1930, exactly thirteen years after the last apparition at Fatima, in a simple pastoral letter, the Bishop of Leiria, Rt. Rev. da Silva, wrote:

"We have pleasure

First: To declare as worthy of credence the visions of the shepherds at the Cova da Iria in the parish of Fatima, of this diocese, on the 13th day of the month from May to October 1917.

Second: To permit officially the devotions to Our Lady of Fatima."

May 13th 1931 saw the Cardinal of Lisbon, together with all the bishops of Portugal, consecrate their country to the Immaculate Heart of Mary. This took place in the Cova da Iria, before some 300,000 spectators.

Lucy had much to be pleased about, especially as her vocation of spreading devotion to the Immaculate Heart of Mary seemed to be gaining momentum. Her euphoria, however, did not last, for by 1935 Russia remained unconsecrated and promotion officially of the First Five Saturdays was negligible. In a letter dated January 21st

Sister Lucy, Fatima, 1967, Golden Jubilee of Apparitions

1935 to her confessor, Father Gonçalves, Lucy had this to say.

".....Regarding the matter of Russia; about 3 years ago Our Lord was very displeased because his request had not been attended to, and I made the fact known to the bishop in a letter. Up to date, Our Lord has asked nothing more of me except prayers and sacrifices."

How difficult it was to get anything done about Russia! Not only had Lucy to convince the hierarchy that these messages were authentic; it was necessary also to reassure herself on this matter.

Her mental anguish showed in a letter of May 29th 1936 to her confessor.

"If I am not mistaken, the good Lord promises to end the persecution in Russia, if the Holy Father himself will make a solemn act of reparation and consecration of Russia to the Sacred Hearts of Jesus and Mary, as well as ordering all the bishops of the world to do the same. The Holy Father must then promise that, upon the ending of this persecution, he will approve and recommend the practice of the reparatory devotion of the First Five Saturdays.

"I declare being very much afraid of making a mistake, and the cause of this fear is the fact that I did not see Our Lord personally, but only felt his divine presence.

"About the repugnance I have of telling this to Reverend Mother Superior. I do not know exactly where it comes from; it may be partly fear that she will disapprove of all this, or say that it is an illusion, or a suggestion of the devil and things of that sort...."

A major difficulty was to get every bishop in the world to take part in a solemn act of consecration, but Lucy explained this as part of a divine plan.

"....Not very long ago I asked Our Lord why he would not convert Russia without the Holy Father making the consecration."

"*Because I want my whole Church to acknowledge the*

consecration as a triumph of the Immaculate Heart of Mary, so that it may extend its cult later on and put devotion to this Immaculate Heart beside devotion to My Sacred Heart."

"But, my God," I said, "the Holy Father probably won't believe me unless you yourself move him with a special inspiration."

"The Holy Father. Pray very much for the Holy Father. He will do it, but it will be too late. Nevertheless the Immaculate Heart of Mary will save Russia. It has been entrusted to her."

The strange light prophesied by Mary, and later known to astronomers as the Aurora Borealis, made its appearance on the night of January 25th 1938. Seen all over Europe, it was given wide coverage in national papers the next day. In its wake followed the heightened atrocities of the Spanish Civil War and the Second World War.

The war figured prominently in Lucy's correspondence. Her letters contain precious insights into the nature of God's justice and mercy.

"I regret that, despite the urgings of the Holy Spirit, (I am speaking of Russia and the Immaculate Heart of Mary) the opportunity was allowed to slip by. Our Lord also laments this. Because of this act he would have restrained his justice and pardoned the world, (delivering it) from the scourge of war, which, from Spain, Russia is promoting throughout the nations."

Another letter brings in a very interesting and vital new topic, namely, the protection granted Portugal because of its consecration to the Immaculate Heart.

"Regarding the consecration of Russia. The Holy Father will not do it now. He doubts the reality and he is right. Through some prodigy Our Good Lord could clearly demonstrate that he is the one who is asking for this. But he is using this time to punish the world by means of his justice for so many crimes, and to prepare it for a more complete return to himself. The proof he gives is the special

Pope Paul VI praying before the statue of the crowned Virgin, 1967

protection of the Immaculate Heart granted to Portugal (in World War II), in return for the consecration that was made to her."

The war, however, brought with it a greater urgency in those sympathetic to Lucy's cause. During the September 1939 pilgrimage to Fatima the devotion of the First Five Saturdays was officially made public; following this the Portuguese hierarchy in a collective pastoral urged its people about the necessity of expiation for the sins of mankind.

Meanwhile, various approaches were made to the Pope about Russia being consecrated; Lucy was recommended to write to him personally. Before setting down to do so she asked the advice of Our Lord exposed in the Blessed Sacrament; there she received this extraordinary locution.

"Pray for the Holy Father, sacrifice yourself so that his courage does not succumb under the bitterness that oppresses him. The tribulation will continue and augment. I will punish the nations for their crimes, by war, famine, and persecution of my Church and this will lie heavily upon my vicar on earth. His Holiness will obtain an abbreviation of these days of tribulation if he takes heed of my wishes by promulgating the act of consecration of the whole world to the Immaculate Heart of Mary, with a special mention of Russia..."

Here God's compassion and mercy is very much to the fore. No longer is he insistent upon the co-operation of the world's bishops in order to bring about a speedy end to the war. Instead he asks the Pope alone to consecrate the world to Mary's Immaculate Heart, with a special mention of Russia.

This he did on October 31st 1942 in the silver jubilee year of the apparitions at Fatima.

Torchlight Procession

"STOP OFFENDING GOD FOR HE IS ALREADY MUCH OFFENDED"

The Second World War was ended, and even though both America and Germany did all they could to involve her, Portugal remained neutral. Not one alien set foot on their territory, even though a German armoured division at one time advanced into San Sebastian.

The protection granted the country was proof enough of Mary's power. "It was also," wrote Lucy, "a reward for the prayers and penance offered up each month at Fatima."

We understood her meaning when, on the morning of the 12th from our vantage point near the roundabout whose roads branch off to Ourem and Santarem, we watched the pilgrims come.

What an eye opener this proved to be! They walked in groups, stocky hard working peasants, young and old alike, footsore, travel stained, weary. The women dressed more or less similarly, in either 'all black', or floral patterned dirndl skirts topped with blouses and shawls. On their 'kerchief covered heads they balanced an assortment of odd shaped bundles. These contained blankets, cooking utensils, food, in fact anything necessary for a journey. The men, wearing dark work-a-day clothes, staffs in hand, walked ahead. Not one pair of walking shoes was in evidence; on the contrary most had bare feet; just a few sported home-made slippers or flip-flops.

Each person carried rosary beads in their hands, and they said the prayers.

By mid afternoon all roads to Fatima were packed with pilgrims making for the Cova da Iria. With respects paid to Our Lady in the Capelhina, as the chapel of the apparitions is affectionately called, preparations were made for their all night vigil. Beneath the trees surrounding this vast esplanade, they spread blankets; some pilgrims sat and ate a frugal meal, others snatched an hour's sleep, the rest unable to bear wasting time pushed themselves to the limit: on their knees along the hard gravel ground, travelling three quarters of a mile, from one end of the Cova to the Capelhina, breaking backs, blood stained knees and toes. Old ladies unwilling to give up were helped towards the goal by their younger counterparts. Soldiers in cotton battledress did it the hard way; they propelled themselves along on their elbows.

Competition? Exhibitionism? No, not at all, there were no smiles or laughter, this was penitence to the full; lips moved constantly in silent prayer and tears glistened in the eyes of most.

At 11 p.m. some 300,000 pilgrims lit candles which they were to take in procession; the basilica with its huge outside altar was illuminated and the Fatima 'Ave' rang out.

Faces became animated as the graceful statue of Our Lady, on a golden bier banked with pink and white carnations, left the Capelhina and was carried shoulder high around the Cova; after which the bearers replaced it.

Midnight Mass and exposition on the exterior altar took us through to the dawn Masses, when various penitential exercises re-started.

At 11 a.m. came a change of atmosphere; Our Lady was on the move again! Tiny tots, dressed to resemble angels, spread flower petals in her path, until at the altar she came to rest and remained for solemn High Mass. All too soon it ended. Forging a way through, our Queen in procession made for the Capelhina. Handkerchiefs formed a sea of white, and pilgrims, tears streaming down their faces, waved farewell. Our voices joined with theirs in singing the 'Adeus'.

Dear Lady of the Rosary, our pilgrimage is ending, our way must be wending with memories in our hearts. With memories and longings, and gratitude and gladness and endings of sadness because we must part.

One final request as our handkerchiefs we wave, Oh help us always our own and all souls to save.

With Our Lady's statue back in its place, the Domain cleared as if by magic. Pilgrims hastening back to their work in the fields, left quietly and orderly, exactly as they had arrived.

Thus closed the October celebrations of 1975. At the opening ceremony of 1976 one point two million people were present, many of whom had spent best part of the week travelling on foot. Undoubtedly a lot of people, and, one would say, it shows some measure of the love and confidence they have in Our Lady. This was further emphasised during the communist disturbances. Someone who happened to be in Fatima when these disturbances were at their height in 1975, had this to say:

"On May 13th, every bishop of Portugal was present at Fatima, and the bishops in fact re-consecrated Portugal to the Immaculate Heart of Mary....each one, on his own, came up to the microphone and read the words of consecration itself...there was quite a lot of people here...over a million...that's probably because the political situation was so tight. But a very strange thing happened. When the bishops were reading out the words of consecration, a woman's voice came over the microphone with every bishop as he spoke, saying exactly the same words. I took this myself to be the press or television...the world of communications...I took it to be something like this...the whole thing was televised from start to finish. But they've been looking into it since. It was no one from T.V. and they cannot trace the source of the voice, and now they're beginning to think it was some supernatural or divine intervention...but, y'know...one just doesn't know...but it makes you think..."

The prophecy given in 1920 by Jacinta when she was in hospital at Lisbon goes as follows:

"Our Lady is profoundly indignant over the sins committed in Portugal. For this reason a terrible catacylsm of a social disorder threatens our country, principally the city of Lisbon. It appears a civil war of an anarchist or

Communist nature will break out, accompanied by sacking, assasinations, fires and devastation of every sort. The capital will turn into a real image of hell."

Is it possible that this prophecy referred to the 1975 Communist coup, and if so, was its suppression due to those who responded to Our Lady's requests, for which her protection was a reward?

In the meantime Russia spreads its errors throughout the world, promoting wars and persecutions, just as Mary predicted in 1917, the same year when in St. Petersburg atheistic Communism was planned and launched. Since then its advance has been dramatic and its influence both politically and militarily has never been stronger. Today it looms over the West like a sword of Damocles with the might of manpower and sophisticated weaponry to over-run it at will.

Lucy had no illusions that Russia could be used as the instrument of God's wrath.

"God wishes that the Bishops of Spain unite themselves in retreat and determine a reform in people, clergy and religious orders, some convents and many members of others!...Do you understand? He wishes that it be made clear to the souls that the penance he now wants and requires consists, first of all, in the sacrifice that each must make to fulfil his own religious and worldly duties. He promises the end of the war shortly in answer to the act of consecration made by His Holiness. But since it was incomplete, the conversion of Russia will take place later. If the Bishops of Spain do not attend to his wishes, it will be once more the scourge with which God punishes them...."

The fact that Communism gains in power and influence is in itself a pressure gauge of God's wrath. The reform demanded has not taken place.

In Lisbon the Mother of God told Jacinta that it is sins of impurity which most destroy man and send souls to hell; luxuries too must be avoided. In other words she.

Chapel of Apparitions, May 13th, 1975

condemned the overt adherence and misuse of both sex and possessions.

The high standard of living in developed countries has meant the enjoyments of life are available to most. This is not to say they are bad or indeed that we have no right to them; it is simply man's excessive attachment and greed which has turned them into false idols. In fact so few people can appreciate the good and lovely things of the world without being taken over by them. Most reprehensible to Our Lord are those who ought to know better, particularly the clergy and religious whose vows have not resulted in a life of sacrifice and detachment from worldly things.

"Our good Lord and Our Heavenly Mother frequently complain about the sinful life of the majority of people, even those who call themselves practising Catholics. But above all they complain heavily of the lukewarm, indifferent and extremely comfortable lives of most of the priests and male and female religious. The number of souls that come to them in sacrifice and in an intimate life of love is small and very limited."

Lucy's letter is also compassionate; she continues:

"These things that are confided to me break my heart, especially since I am one of those unfaithful souls. Our Lord does not spare me. He reveals to me the mountain of my imperfections, which I admit with confusion. In spite of all Our Lord continues to communicate himself to my soul."

And elsewhere:

"The worst is that I'm among the lukewarm, despite the efforts he has made to include me among the fervent. I promise with great ease, but I falter with even greater ease. Dust adheres to actions as it does to clothes without our knowing how it got there. But he is patient, which is fortunate for me. He wants me to live in heaven but I continually attach myself more to the earth."

Higher wages and lessening of working hours has also

made people more vunerable to the dissipation that comes from easy living; abuse of sex figures prominently in this. Sex shops have proliferated and the widest selection of pornography openly flaunted in newspaper shops is available to all, including children. Daily papers cannot exist without their nudes, while 'X rated' films are the norm. Rape has increased, so has violence and disrespect of the person; though unprecedented it is not the unexpected outcome of pornography. A most eminent clinical psychologist specialising in psyco-sexual problems, was sure enough of his facts to fly from America, stand up in court and claim without equivocation that "Yes, pornography or near pornography corrupts, and I've proved it."

A very strong link exists between exposure to this matter and the conduct of people he had examined after offences involving rape and murder. He is particularly worried about the effect of freely available pornography, for since it has been on open sale the number of sex attacks has risen.

"I find it very disheartening," he said, "to see society regress from a highly civilised level back into the primitive state where we began life. We have let sex get out of proportion in our lives. We are in danger of throwing away all we have created in our search for a higher form of life."

A 15 year old boy sat through two sex films and one of violence. Within hours of leaving the cinema he knifed a complete stranger. The lawyer in charge said, "People call these sort of films works of art, and describe the participants as geniuses....there must have been a connection between what the actor did on the screen and what operated in the boy's mind because it happened so soon after he had seen the films."

The habit of sinning, which Our Lady spoke to Jacinta about when referring to the sins that most offend God, is such that it is now difficult to tell the difference between right and wrong.

Killing un-born babies is regarded as a form of *birth control* and euthanasia comes under the polite euphemism, *mercy killing*. The word 'sin' or 'sinner' is looked upon as a dirty word on no account to be used.

There have been many descriptions of the present state of society. The following is as good as any:

"Many of us don't call ourselves penitents, we say we're patients; we don't call ourselves sinners, we say we're sick; we don't bother to confess to a priest, we go to a psychiatrist. When there's a burglary in the street we don't call it a sin, it's a crime. So when you're unhappy, when you're discouraged, full of despair, crying, nervous, lonely and empty, you seek a natural explanation to a spiritual disorder. That's why we don't think we're sinners. We think in terms of nurses, doctors, drugs and tranquillisers."

An authority on Fatima sees its message as particularly relevant to our times.

"If there's a riot or a disturbance anywhere, millions of dollars and pounds are spent to find out the cause of the disturbance, the city riot and all these mixed up things, and the real reason is that the soul is disturbed and in a state of sin, and it manifests itself through violence. Jacinta hit at the root of all evil; you must convert the soul. When that's transformed as she was transformed, what a different world this would be!"

Our Lady promised the world peace when Russia is consecrated, and not until then. Regularly the Pope is petitioned to do this in the manner requested. It has not been done. Again in an interview, we came across what we consider to be the most likely reason.

"The time is not right....just having a consecration....even with all the bishops, in itself doesn't make much sense. They won't have a consecration until we're down on our knees...down on the floor really, and realise that this is the one thing that is going to save us...."

It would seem that we are living in a time not unlike the beginning of the Second World War. Pressure is on for a consecration we neither deserve nor are ready for. The time will come as is pointed out when we are on our knees begging for it, though it will probably take something cataclysmic to turn our minds to God, and then only out of sheer desperation.

Although the eleventh hour is here, though some would maintain we are already living on borrowed time, it is not too late to amend our lives and beg pardon for our sins. The protection given Portugal shows how God's justice can be tempered by his mercy, that chastisement can be averted by prayer and penance, the power of which that country gives ample testimony.

Pilgrimage Day, Cova da Iria

"MY IMMACULATE HEART WILL LEAD YOU TO GOD".

Fatima is above all a love story. It tells of three youngsters who were completely overwhelmed by love; it changed them, and that meant everything changed. The parties, music, dancing, festas, and rough and tumble games on the threshing floor all became meaningless and empty. They were swept off their feet by love and it bore them along relentlessly. Mary started them on the road when she got them to think of others.

The prayers and penances she asked for were not for themselves. Suddenly the whole world was their concern. In each apparition Our Lady insisted, *Pray the rosary every day so that the war will come to an end.* She also said, *Continue saying it that the world may have peace.*

The sacrifices she demanded they make were for the benefit of sinners who have no one to plead for them.

In thinking less about themselves the three little ones were better able to spread Our Lady's messages. They became courageous and fearless, overcoming every obstacle. Unaffected by wagging tongues and ridicule they were brave enough to reprimand adults where necessary.

Francisco, by nature a loner, turned this to good by devoting his short life to private prayer in order to console the all too often offended and neglected God.

Jacinta, dominant and strong-willed, used these qualities for making unceasing sacrifices.

Lucy's job was to stay on earth and spread devotion to Our Lady's Immaculate Heart: first she learnt to read and write. Now her memoirs written in obedience furnish the world with delightful insights into their lives; her letters propogate her cause.

The children teach us the importance of each day: how prayers, works, sufferings and joys–in fact every moment of life–can be offered up to God to help save the world. An apostle of Fatima insists; "Say your morning offering, by your morning offering of reparation to the Immaculate Heart of Mary... by that small but powerful morning offering of reparation, every act you do becomes a sacrifice because the word sacrifice means to make holy. Every act is a sacrifice because you've made it so by your morning offering....every cup of coffee, tearing your hair out at the kids, doing a job well, the aggravations and irritations, in fact all that you do, gives the graces for the conversion of sinners....if you don't make your morning offering you've wasted the day as far as grace is concerned."

"Bless yourself, make your morning offering," he repeats, "love Our Lady, say your daily rosary, become a daily communicant, visit Our Lord in the Blessed Sacrament, make time to get away on your own, even for five minutes so that you can clear your mind....but above all STOP OFFENDING GOD AND AMEND YOUR WAYS."

At Fatima Mary showed her Heart surrounded by thorns. Because we have hurt her Son, we have hurt her; because we offend Him we offend her. In making reparation to her Immaculate Heart, we are also making reparation to Our Lord's Sacred Heart. And in turning to her, what she said to Lucy applies to us all;

"My Immaculate Heart will be your refuge, and the road that will lead you to God."

ACT OF CONSECRATION TO THE IMMACULATE HEART OF MARY

I, N..............., a faithless sinner, renew and ratify today in thy heart, O Immaculate Mother, the vows of my Baptism; I renounce forever Satan, his pomps and works; and I give myself entirely to Jesus Christ, the Incarnate Wisdom, to carry my cross after Him all the days of my life and to be more faithful to Him than I have ever been before.

In the presence of all the Heavenly Court I choose thee this day for my mother and mistress. I deliver and consecrate to Thee as Thy slave my body and soul, my goods both interior and exterior, and even the value of all my good actions, past, present and future; leaving to Thee entirely and fully the right of disposing of me without exception according to Thy good pleasure for the greater glory of God in time and in eternity.

Amen

MORNING OFFERING

Oh, Jesus through the most Immaculate Heart of Mary, I offer you all my prayers, works, sufferings and joys of this day, for all the intentions of your Divine Heart in the Holy Mass.

EPILOGUE

After the major celebrations of the 12th and 13th, the Cova da Iria is deserted. All one can hear is an occasional metalic click from the boot of a sanctuary guard on the basilica steps. This is hardly surprising, for Fatima is far removed from the main highways of Europe and very much a shrine of the Portuguese people. But its very bareness only accentuates a presence. There is no doubting that She is there.

At Lourdes we thought of her as a tender mother whose winning smile in each of the eighteen apparitions did so much to make Bernadette feel at home. Fatima, somehow, was different. The hauntingly sad and grave face of the statue depicting Our Lady of Fatima followed us wherever we went. This shrine had an urgency and seriousness about it, the like of which we had never encountered. We could not help thinking that one of the most prodigious miracles known to history took place here. Mary had come as a powerful queen compelling the attention of her children, not to ask but to command:

"Stop offending God, for he is already much offended"

The means she gave us to amend our lives were prayer and penance. But the prayer and penance she asks for are not for ourselves but for others. Just at the seers prayed for something that seemed wrong to be righted or for a person whose actions were not all they should be, so Mary tells us to do the same.

Our obligations and responsibilities, however, extend further afield. What is wrong with our country, for instance, what is unjust or even evil about its laws? Its people? These should be the matter of our prayers. Likewise, for peace in the world; the conversion of Russia.

It is as if in a very real sense God's hands are tied. What he wishes for the world cannot come about without our co-operation. As sacrifices save sinners, so prayers can bring about wonders. Even if we were not to venture beyond one room, we can be a power for good in our country, in the world. These truths are obvious, but to our shame it needed Fatima to remind us.

ADDENDUM

THE FATIMA PRAYERS

THE ANGEL'S PRAYERS:

My God, I believe, I adore, I hope and I love you. I beg pardon for those who do not believe, do not adore, do not hope and do not love you.

Most Holy Trinity, Father, Son and Holy Spirit, I offer you the most precious body and blood, soul and divinity of Jesus Christ present in all the tabernacles of the earth, in reparation for the outrages and indifferences with which He Himself is offended. And through the infinite merits of His Most Sacred Heart and of the Immaculate Heart of Mary, I beg of you the conversion of poor sinners.

OUR LADY'S PRAYERS:

Oh Jesus, forgive us our sins, save us from the fires of hell; lead all souls to heaven especially those in most need.
(To be said after each decade of the rosary).

Jesus, it is for love of you, for the conversion of sinners and in reparation for sins committed against the Immaculate Heart of Mary.
(To be said when making a sacrifice)